Estranged

Amra Mitrovska

Published by Amra Mitrovska, Woodridge, Illinois

First Print Edition in the United States of America by Amra Mitrovska, 2025

Library of Congress Control Number: 2025924165

ISBN Paperback: 979-8-9939117-1-7

ISBN Hardback: 979-8-9939117-2-4

ISBN E-book: 979-8-993117-0-0

Editor: Aldiana Pehlivanović Deumić (authoraldiana.com)

Book Cover Co-Designer: Selma Muminović

Formatting: Alina Rubin of Hearts and Sails Author Services (heartsandsails.com)

DEDICATION

I dedicate this book to every soul that, even for a moment, felt like a stranger in their own life.

To those who have wandered in silence, longing for their voice to be heard, for their truth to take shape in the world.

To all who have carried the weight of not belonging— may these pages remind you that you were never truly alone.

ACKNOWLEDGEMENT

To those who carried pieces of me when I could not carry them myself.

To **Aldiana Pehlivanović Deumić,** whose insightful guidance and editorial care helped me shape my voice.

To **European Service LLC**, **your trusted partner in home care!** Proudly providing exceptional care and support to seniors across Illinois, with a team of skilled and compassionate caregivers you can truly trust. Thank you for believing in my work — beyond all business titles and roles.

To **Martin**, **Elena**, and **Nikolija** — your laughter, your love, your patience gave this book its heartbeat.

To **Bosnia**, with its scars and tenderness, and to **Chicago**, with its skyline of new beginnings — you are both my home.

And to everyone who opens these pages, may you find a reflection of your own courage here.

Contents

Chapter 1

The Crisis in Yugoslavia
Donji Vakuf, Bosnia and Herzegovina, 1986

What would you have done if you had known that the war in Bosnia and Herzegovina would drag on for years?

Do you have memories you would like to forget, or those you want to remember, thirty years later?

What choices would you have made?

Dall never hoped that time in Bosnia and Herzegovina would one day be divided into before and after the war.

Nor was it hers to think—such kinds of worries belonged to adults.

This is the story of a nameless child, the story of "the others," the never-spoken truth of the invisible victims of the Bosnian war—children born of mixed marriages.

Dall was only eight years old at the beginning of the '90s, when signs of some new time arrived. For her age a tiny, undernourished girl, with a big and broad smile, she had no idea that she would spend the most beautiful childhood in a basement.

Bosnia and Herzegovina, Dall's homeland, stood as both the primal guardian and the beating heart of Yugoslavhood, and while the SFRY lived, its people—people like us—carried the name Yugoslavs with a quiet, instinctive pride. The SFRY was large and powerful.

It was a republic in the very heart of Europe, based exclusively on the concept of brotherhood and unity. Yugoslavia was founded on the remnants of the Turkish Empire and the Austro-Hungarian Monarchy. As such, it was a safe refuge and a mother to all the inhabitants of that cultural circle.

The country was wonderfully diverse. Under one government, Bosnians, Slovenes, Serbs, Montenegrins, Macedonians, Croatians, Albanians, Romanians, and other national minorities lived together in harmony.

The inhabitants of the former Yuga, as it was fondly called among the people, enjoyed free healthcare and schooling, a paid one-month annual vacation, they had regular salaries and the unemployment rate was minimal.

In one word—they had a normal standard of living. People belonged to the middle class, which existed then, and they were not divided into rich and poor.

In May of 1980, with the death of Josip Broz Tito, the former president of Yugoslavia, the country stepped into a period of economic crisis that brought inflation, led to unemployment, and hurled the economy—which had once flourished—into certain ruin.

However, we can say with certainty that the collapse of the economy, the oil crisis, and even the large amounts of foreign debts were not the only reasons for the breakup of Yugoslavia.

The dinar, the currency of that time, was falling faster than inflation.

The enemy of Yugoslavia was not the great powers of the West, as many like to say, but rather cultural and religious differences which, without a doubt, caused division among the ethnic groups in the country.

Nationalism.

Human stupidity, and hatred rooted for years, did not withstand the utopia called national consciousness.

That seed was sown sometime long ago, generations back, and in time those came who reaped the fruits—manipulating the popular masses, because they knew and were able to.

Dall grew up celebrating Christmases, Easters, Eids, Prvi Maj or Labor Day, as well as any other state holiday or celebratory day that was marked in the neighborhood. The people of that region easily found any reason or occasion for celebration.

Those were her most beautiful memories—memories from a time in which similarities and differences among people, as well as their religious affiliations, were equally respected.

Accordingly, Dall never felt belonging nor the need to align herself with some national mass.

Some would simply call that an identity crisis of the Yugoslav people, and Dall was simply too young to understand any of that or, indeed, to attach any significance to it.

Mixed marriages in the former Yugoslavia were, in a way—let us say—desired and encouraged; in any case, they were "normal" among most of the population.

That fateful year 1992 brought a completely different perception, in which those same marriages—from desirable—became despised.

Dall was of mixed blood, the daughter of a Muslim Bosnian father and an Orthodox mother. In those years, children like her—born between two worlds—were quietly placed in the category of the "others."

The others were exposed to insults among children, often asked: Where did you get such a name, with a Muslim father and an Orthodox mother? As nationally uncommitted, they encountered many simply hushed-up problems—as if they had never even existed.

Dall grew up with her mother, but the combination of her first and last name, which she received at birth, choosing neither mother nor father, always bothered someone.

Emre—a name of Islamic origin, although Dall did not choose it—bothered her mother's side of the family, and so her mother baptized her, whereby she was given the name Dall, more desirable and more accepted in the circles in which her mother Mira moved.

Mira, for her part, hoped that the holy act itself would

shield her only daughter from the evil eye, and that, through it, others would no longer regard Dall as nationally uncommitted.

The result of that whole—let us call it thus—drama was that Dall at school was registered as Emre, and everywhere else simply as Dall.

The girl was irritated and confused by both; she would have been happiest to be nameless—which would have brought much less talk, polemic, questions, and everything else to which she had no answer.

Her vision of utopia was far from all that—in a small town on the river Vrbas, which was in central Bosnia and bore the name Donji Vakuf.

Dall jealously guarded and nurtured the earliest memories from childhood spent in that town.

Those memories were her escape from reality, into which, as "the other," she often did not fit.

Donji Vakuf was divided into quarters, and the two best-known neighborhoods were Gornja and Donja Mahala—the Upper and Lower parts of town. The word "mahalla," meaning neighborhood, came from Turkish, a reminder of how deeply history shaped even the language we used every day.

Loanword from the Turkish language, brought—as many others were—and adopted in those areas during the Ottoman Empire.

During the rule of the Turks, there were great intertwining's of the two cultures; that led to the adoption of certain words, customs, foods, and architectural styles.

Dall spent her early childhood in Donja Mahala, the lower part of town, where the rhythms of daily life shaped her earliest memories. Donja Mahala was inhabited by a strange mix of Gypsies, Orthodox, and Muslims.

Her mother Mira also spent a good part of her youth in that town, experiencing it as her second home.

Mira was absent most of the time, working for a piece of bread and the costs of caring for Dall, and while Mira lived on the edge of existence, wearing torn stockings—Dall was safe, provided for, and happy.

The patriarchal family that took care of Dall's care were Muslims, and so it is natural that Dall was exposed to their culture and customs.

Mr. Ibro was the head, the pillar of the family; his role was to take care of his wife and children.

He was a strong, middle-aged man of two meters, with great authority in his family—respected by all without exception, despite not being related to Dall by blood.

Ibro was a carpenter, working until three in the afternoon in a nearby company.

At that time, the sound of the siren was associated with something good—for the working class it marked the end of working hours, and for little Dall—happiness.

This was before the war.

She would run as if without a soul down the steep street as soon as the siren sounded, to meet Ibro—the only father figure she had ever known.

Ibro would seize her with strong hands, place her on his shoulders, and carry her home.

Dall's father was out of the picture, living his own life in the nearby town of Gornji Vakuf. After separating from Dall's mother, who was eleven years his junior, he got together with a woman eight years his senior, who had divorced her husband and had two daughters.

She lived on her own terms, in her own apartment, and she managed to endure his shortcomings—his drinking, his long nights away, his sudden absences. Still, they built a life that brought them two daughters, daughters who never wanted to connect with Dall, even though none of them had any part in the choices their parents made.

Dall remembers the times the school needed her father to sign documents. She would call, only for his wife to answer the phone and calmly state that he didn't live there, that he couldn't be reached.

Meanwhile, on the doorstep of Ibro's home, a steaming pan of pie released its warmth into the cool air, slowly settling as it waited for him to return. The air was thick with its scent, teasing hungry little mouths that could hardly wait—restless hands held back until they were washed, hearts eager to gather at the round wooden table, where the first bite would taste like home itself. Ibro's wife, Safa, was a housewife, her life devoted to the children and the keeping of the home. If someone needed a nanny, she would watch other people's children because any additional earnings were always welcome.

Safa was a hardworking, calm woman—one of those, as people say, to whom you could show bloody hands and no one would ever find out. She knew how to keep secrets, and many she took with her to the grave.

Dall was convinced that no one in the world could cook the way Safa did—especially the old traditional dishes, whose recipes had been passed down from lap to lap, generation to generation.

Ibro and Safa had three children—two boys and a girl. Their eldest son already stood with one foot in the world of adults—gentle, blue-eyed, fair-skinned, sincere, and kind-hearted.

The daughter, too, already grown, was a rebel—her beautiful blue eyes shining with the kind of stubbornness only women can truly possess.

The youngest son, Amad, was seven years older than Dall and, as the baby of the family and the one who most resembled his mother, he was Safa's favorite. With hair dark as a pitch-black night and playful brown eyes, he often teased Dall in play, while she trailed after him like a puppy—sometimes to the point of driving him mad. Safa, firm in her ways, would order Amad to keep an eye on Dall whenever they played outside, and the boy, though reluctant to accept the role thrust upon him, carried it out with the quiet seriousness of an older brother, protecting her as best he could.

Be that as it may, a special bond tied them together; though not related by blood, they never felt it any differently. Having been raised together, they regarded each other as siblings. Their family embodied everything Dall herself had been missing: a true home, stability, a father who cared, a house alive with children, and, above all, the love, respect, and mutual understanding that held them close. As there is a reason for everything, it was the turmoil of the Yugoslav crisis—with its unrelenting need for additional income—that led little Dall into their care.

What began as necessity soon revealed itself as a mutual gift: for Dall, the warmth and stability of a family she had yearned for; for them, the extra income that helped carry them through those difficult times. Their old family house stood at the top of a narrow, steep street, and behind it stretched enough space to keep animals, a small world of its own tucked away from the road. Ibro, a quiet and patient man with a deep love for nature, always kept a pair of rabbits and, from time to time, chickens, and goats as well. But it was the pigeons—symbols of peace and love—that were his true passion.

He knew more about them than most, and the flutter of their wings seemed to echo the gentleness of his own spirit. Dall adored feeding the newborn animals with a bottle of milk, and she would lovingly give them names, often inspired by the unique patterns on their fur and skin.

The narrow streets of Donja Mahala were made for children's play and always full of children, and passers-by could get an earful of shrieks, clamor, and cheerful children's laughter.

In that little town on the banks of the Vrbas, a spirit of true togetherness and warmth between the two nations seemed to breathe through every street. With the coming of evening, one could hear laughter and gentle voices drifting from courtyard to courtyard, as if the town itself were woven from harmony, while the night air carried the sweet fragrance of freshly cut grass.

Children would cleverly dream up all sorts of mischief just to snatch an unripe piece of fruit from the yard of their neighbor known as "Patak"—for reasons known only to them, it always seemed to have a special taste. And when someone from the group was caught, the slower ones who failed to escape were met not with anger but with gentle, almost playful reproaches—

offered more with a smile than any real grievance, as if even the scolding itself were simply another part of the game.

In winter, the little rascals turned the narrow street into their playground, carving an ice slide that ran from Ibro's house down to its very end. The bolder ones dared to cross to the other side of the brook—a slender stream that split the street in two. Now and then, a child would tumble into the channel, only to be pulled out by stronger hands, dripping and shivering, yet laughing all the while, their joy rising above the cold.

No one wanted to be a snitch, and so the small—or slightly bigger—mischiefs remained forever hidden from the parents.

The girls made dolls from scraps, cardboard boxes, collected napkins, while the boys oversaw organizing limun i narandža (lemons and oranges), hide-and-seek, tag, dodgeball between two fires, and similar group games that everyone looked forward to. All those were excellently devised games, awakening and nurturing children's imagination, which, unfortunately, no longer exist, because the new generations brought something completely opposite to what Dall and her faithful crew considered beautiful.

In small communities like this one, everyone knew each other, and the older women from the "mahala" would often feed both, their own and other people's children. Thus, it was not unusual to receive a piece of homemade bread spread with pork lard and sprinkled with red paprika from Aunt Dara, or homemade bread sprinkled with sugar from Aunt Zada, a piece of fruit from Aunt Mira, and the like, from any other woman in the neighborhood.

There was not much, and they did not live in abundance, but what people had they gladly shared with their neighbors, living fulfilled and happy in the valley of the river Vrbas.

Dall was a lively, talkative child, yet as she grew, life's circumstances shaped her nature, teaching her far too early how to restrain her feelings and veil them behind carefully chosen filters.

She watched her mother, who lived from paycheck to paycheck, without the support of a husband, struggling to pay the bills.

Daydreaming represented an escape from reality for Dall whenever life dealt her a crushing blow.

She would see herself barefoot, running through fields, free, playing with little goats or sliding on improvised sleds down the steep street, because a child somehow spontaneously and unconsciously gravitates toward memories, objects, or persons it loves.

Those images eased her burdens, for she had grown up in the embrace of a caring, harmonious, and encouraging family. The memory of that warmth became her shield, guarding her against the storms that later rose in the arena of life and with which she was destined to grapple.

If, however, she began to panic, having no solution, she would hear Ibro's voice somewhere in her subconscious, which would gently but strictly scold his youngest son, who enjoyed teasing Dall in play, simply because she was the youngest member of the family.

It was normal for neighbors to visit one another, and Ibro and Safa took Dall as the youngest with them wherever they went as guests. Their children were teenagers, and they had no desire for various sittings in other people's houses.

For Dall, such evenings meant fun and play with some of the children of her age, because almost every house had two or even more children.

Little did Dall know that those very memories would one day become her salvation in the terrible times to come—times marked by the wail of sirens announcing general or air raids, and the deafening detonations of bombs and shells. The most repressed memories that Dall had were tied to the period of leaving Ibro's family.

She remembers little, yet the silence of Ibro and Safa lingers—their hushed voices and heavy glances speaking of costs that kept piling up, of too many mouths to feed. Mira, unable to cover what was needed for Dall, had no choice but to move with her daughter into a shared apartment with Ljuba, her coworker at the time. Life there was modest, and space was scarce, but within those walls Dall learned once more how to adjust, carrying the memory of each change as quietly as the unspoken worries of the adults around her.

Chapter 2

A City Left Behind

Bugojno, Bosnia and Herzegovina, 1987

Mira had always believed that life, no matter how cruel, somehow offered new beginnings. After leaving Donji Vakuf and the safety of Ibro and Safa's household, she and Dall moved to Bugojno—a bigger, noisier town that seemed to swallow them whole. For Dall, nothing there felt like home.

She felt like a stranger in her own skin in that tiny apartment in which nothing belonged to her, nothing had the smell of warmth and home.

She was never deeply tied to the town that slept peacefully in the Skopljanska Valley, distinct from so many Bosnian-Herzegovinian towns born of the Ottoman legacy

Before the war, Bugojno was a multiethnic town, home to roughly equal numbers of Muslims and Catholics, about half as many Orthodox, and others who, like many in that era, identified simply as Yugoslavs.

Bugojno carried a rich past leading the former state in birth rates during the 1980s and standing tall among the most developed industrial towns. In the very heart of Bosnia and Herzegovina, it promised progress and prosperity, far greater than neighboring Donji Vakuf.

But to little Dall, such promise was empty. She cared nothing for rankings or industry—only for the loss of the world she had cherished, the places and bonds she had been torn away from.

Mira worked endlessly, leaving Dall in the care of Ljuba—a woman who never had much tenderness for little girls. Under her watch, Dall grew quiet, closed within herself, carrying a loneliness that slowly hardened into bitterness.

Ljuba had come from the rugged hills of Montenegro. Life had not been gentle with her. She bore a son, Vedran, out of wedlock with an Albanian from Kosovo, and made her living waiting tables, piecing together survival from meager tips. Yet Vedran did not grow up by her side. He was taken in by Ljuba's sister and brother-in-law, a couple denied children of their own, who welcomed him as a long-awaited blessing. They held him in the embrace Ljuba herself could not fully offer.

For little Dall, it was a time of despair and uncertainty, memories she recalls only with reluctance. Deep within, she held her mother, Mira, responsible for not finding a way for them to remain in Ibro's house. She blamed her for the heaviness that pressed upon her chest, even as she knew it was not truly her fault—that such blame was unjust, even cruel. But children need someone to hold accountable, and so Mira became the face of all that loss—not because she deserved it, but because love was closest at hand.

That buried anger pressed against her small being until it spilled out in defiance. She began to misbehave, as if rebellion could shield her from helplessness. The rage and frustration became her armor, a raw defense mechanism that gave her both strength and energy. And in time, that same force became what pushed her to adapt, to bend with the new reality instead of breaking beneath it.

Dall would hide in corners as Lyba called, left half-eaten food and dirty dishes in the corners, or ruined her lipsticks—small, deliberate acts that gave voice to her silent pain. Over time, she learned to bow to what could not be changed. She tried to be good, slowly grasping that the world did not spin solely around her pain, and that her mother, of all people, bore the least blame for any of it.

Dall had always carried a sharpened intuition, an instinct beyond her years. She sensed early on how a wounded mind could shape and even shackle a person, and so she began to step back from anything that stirred unease within her. It was her quiet way of survival— choosing distance over despair.

Mira was born in a small village not far from Bugojno, a place rooted in its own rhythms and traditions. The villagers were mostly Orthodox, people who had little knowledge of the faiths and customs beyond their own, for the world outside rarely touched them. Like many families of that time, they had children in abundance— partly because contraception was scarce, partly because every extra pair of hands lightened the labor of the fields and the home, and partly because religion praised the gift of life.

Children were viewed less as mouths to feed and more as strength for the household—girls and boys alike woven into the fabric of work. But if a daughter was born, her path usually narrowed to two choices: marry and build a family of her own, or, as the elders said with a shrug, "go with her stomach for bread," leave home to find a future elsewhere.

So, it was with Mira. Still a teenager, she left her village to help care for the children of a married couple her parents knew in town. By sixteen, she was already working in a restaurant, shouldering the weight of adult life before she was fully grown. And it was there, amid the hum of clattering plates and the murmurs of conversation, that she met Sajo—Dall's father. He was older, with dark hair streaked by the first threads of gray, piercing blue eyes, and the kind of quiet confidence that drew attention without effort.

Handsome, intelligent, sure of himself—he seemed like a man who knew exactly where he was going.

The untold story of Dall's mother carries the quiet resonance of triumph. Whatever trials life placed in her path; she rose above them unbeaten. The obstacles she faced did not define her—they only tempered her spirit and sharpened her resolve, leaving behind the echo of a woman who endured, unbroken and unbowed.

Sajo, Dall's father, was a man of contradictions. Charismatic and magnetic, he was an extremely gifted soccer player—well-educated and quick-witted, with thoughts that always raced ahead of others, leaving his peers struggling to keep pace. In company, he shone effortlessly; his openness and charm drew people in, winning their admiration without him ever needing to seek it. But brilliance came with shadows.

A funny story follows him from high school, when he was taken to play for a soccer team in Croatia. Instead of focusing on the game, he and a hometown teammate partied and drank until his older brother came to check on him. Asked to show him the high school, he wandered in circles before admitting he had no idea where they were. And just like that, his soccer career in Croatia ended—before it even had the chance to begin.

His greatest weakness was alcohol, and with it, the inability to remain steady in a relationship. Emotional loyalty and constancy were things he could never offer. He seemed to carry the thought, half-serious and half-mocking: *why tie oneself to one woman when one could have them all?*

He would come and go whenever fate took him to see his daughter, and Dall lived for those moments, simply hoping that this time he would stay longer, be better if she tried harder, showed that she was smart, obedient, and well-behaved, that she could take care of herself, and stay away from all trouble.

Hope dies last, and of course, that never actually happened. Dall grew distrustful, wary of others, and learned early to carry her weight without ever becoming a burden to her mother. She did her best to remain invisible, to slip through life without drawing attention.

Estranged.

She carried an almost bitter resentment toward the people who looked after her during those first fragile years of elementary school. To her, they were not comfort, but reminders of absence—poor replacements for the love and warmth she longed for.

Her mother, Mira, worked across the border in Croatia, driven there by the economic stagnation that had gripped Yugoslavia. Dall understood it was out of necessity, but as a child she felt only the empty chair at dinner, the missing hand to hold on the way to school. Loneliness pressed in from every side.

She watched other children run into the arms of their parents after school, laughing, carefree, unafraid. She longed for that same embrace, yet learned to keep quiet, to swallow her longing so it would not weigh heavier on Mira's already burdened shoulders.

The absence shaped her. It made her cautious with trust, reluctant to lean on anyone, and deeply aware— too early—of how fragile security really was.

In the 1980s, Yugoslavia had fallen into the hands of socialist gangsters. After Tito's death, there was no one left to keep the directors of state enterprises—or the thieves in their ranks—in check. Once the guard was gone, the plundering began. Like mice emboldened by the absence of the cat, they siphoned vast sums from state companies and tucked the money safely into foreign accounts.

Amid this unraveling, Mira and Dall moved once more. Just before Dall began elementary school, they rented the first floor of an old house in the very center of town. The walls were worn, but they offered a roof, a corner of stability in a country quietly sinking.

Their landlady was an older woman named Paula— distant, not easily approached. Yet Dall's childlike intuition whispered there was no danger, that beneath the stern exterior lay something softer.

So, she moved carefully, step by step, testing the edges of Paula's reserve. With small gestures, quiet patience, and the simple honesty only a child can bring, she began to win her trust.

As a child, Dall sensed—deep down—that Paula was a woman marked by loneliness and hurt. Guided by that intuition, she spoke to her openly and offered help in small but deliberate ways: running errands to the store, lending a hand with the cleaning.

Gradually, Paula's reserve softened. Almost without realizing it, she grew attached to the little girl, gladly keeping her company whenever Mira was away.

Paula's house bordered that of the Orthodox priest, Milan. He had a son, Dean, just a year older than Dall. It wasn't long before the two children forged a friendship. With Dean at her side, Dall brightened. No longer the solitary little girl, her small heart began to cast sparks of light into the shadows of her past.

One gloomy autumn day, Dall stood her ground and defended Dean from a group of mischievous neighborhood boys. She had always hated injustice, and something fierce inside her burned with the need to protect those who couldn't fight for themselves.

From that moment on, the two were inseparable flying through the city streets on their bicycles like restless spirits, racing over the lamellas, tumbling into adventures, and slipping into small troubles only children could find.

Dean was a chubby yet gentle boy, his shyness wrapped in a smile and cheeks that blushed easily. Each day he wore a hand-knitted sweater, each one stitched in a different pattern, as if his quiet strength was dressed in softness.

While Dean moved slowly, almost sluggishly—careful in every step, never exerting more effort than necessary—Dall was his complete opposite: impatient, quick-tempered, always a spark ahead of herself.

She was slender and wiry, with curious chocolate- brown eyes that could never stay still. Silence was foreign to her; she carried within her a restless need to set crooked rivers straight, brimming with boundless energy.

Together, Dean and Dall became true partners in play. Most of their days were spent outdoors, returning home with scraped knees, bruises, and small cuts—the visible stamps of childhood, proof of lessons learned the rough way.

Perhaps it was this friendship, its innocence and closeness, that planted the seed in Mira's heart—the thought that her daughter, too, should be baptized.

Dall's memory of the ceremony is hazy, like a faded photograph. She recalls her godmother—Mira's colleague from Montenegro, Ljuba—standing beside her. Even her grandmother Jela, a figure she seldom saw, was there that day.

Godmother Ljuba came from a large family in Nikšić. She had left Montenegro in search of a better life, something her homeland at that time could not provide.

In Bosnia, she worked at a modest pastry shop run by Aki, a Kosovar whose cakes were crafted not for indulgence, but for survival. Over time, Ljuba grew close to Aki, and what began as a working relationship slowly turned into something more personal. From that bond came a son, Vedran, who was quite a bit older than Dall.

What Dall remembered most about him were his large, soulful eyes and the waves of dark hair that framed his face.

Vedran lived with his biological aunt, Ruža, in a spacious house that had once belonged to her husband Luka, the old Bugojno stonemason, perched at the very edge of town. Mira and Dall visited them several times, always in the company of godmother Ljuba.

The last summer before a new school year began, Paula and Dall spent the season with Mira in Croatia.

They stayed in the hotel where Mira worked, savoring long days of sunshine, walks along the beach, the taste of seafood fresh from the sea, and the sweetest children's treat of hot summer days—ice cream.

For Dall, it was a small paradise. She built sandcastles that toppled with the tide, laughed freely, and struck up conversations with tourists from faraway countries, her curious nature shining.

Paula, however, worried. She often remarked—with a mixture of concern and unease—that Dall was too open, too trusting. "One day," she said, "a sweet- talking stranger might carry her off. A heart so exposed will cost her dearly in life."

And perhaps, in part, Paula was right. It was the calm before the storm.

Chapter 3

A Fragile Peace

Bugojno, Bosnia and Herzegovina, 1988

T he late 1980s brought a deepening crisis to Yugoslavia. Factories slowed, jobs disappeared, and a cloud of uncertainty hung over families everywhere. Mira carried the weight of it daily, doing everything she could to keep their small household afloat, shielding Dall from the harshest edges of that reality.

Yet even in such times, she noticed how quick her daughter was. At just six years old, Dall could already read and write in Latin script and perform simple calculations. Mira's pride in her child grew stronger with each passing day, and she became convinced that such gifts should not be left idle. So, she decided to enroll Dall in school a year early, as a volunteer.

Mira's pride in her child grew stronger with each passing day and she became convinced that such gifts should not be left idle. She decided to enroll Dall in school a year early as a volunteer.

She believed this would give her daughter an advantage—an outlet for her energy and a way to secure a brighter future at a time when the world around them seemed increasingly uncertain. On paper, Dall was ready: she passed every test with ease.

But emotionally, she was still too young. Later, they would both realize that the decision, though born of love and hope, had not been the right one.

Dall's first school year was difficult, filled with challenges she could not easily overcome. And then, on that sultry September night, during dinner, an uneasy feeling washed over her—the first instinctive recognition of death's presence. Dall suddenly blurted out: "Aunt Paula will die."

Mira was stunned, her eyes filling with sorrow and fear. She scolded Dall gently, but with an unease in her voice, not knowing how to respond to words that swept through their small house like a cold wind. To this day, Dall remains unsure how she sensed that something terrible would happen to Paula. But the very next morning, Paula sent her out to run a few errands, and when Dall returned, she saw paramedics and unfamiliar people gathered in their front yard. Paula was gone forever.

The silence that followed weighed heavier than any words. Grief for her beloved Aunt Paula, as she always called her, drove Dall to Dean—her silent sanctuary amid the chaos of her sorrow. She ran to his door, heart pounding, as if speed could outrun the pain.

Dall stood in front of the gray, somber house, staring into its empty window frames as though they were doors to an unknown world without Dean. Her heart pounded heavily, her thoughts crashing like waves— "Why did they leave? Didn't I deserve at least a goodbye? Has everything I had now turned to dust?"

She felt grief tightening in her chest, as if some invisible hand pressed down and refused to let go. Tears began to well, but she swallowed them—she didn't want to show weakness, she didn't want anyone to see how broken her heart was.

In that moment, she remembered all those carefree days with Dean—their laughter, bike races, and countless adventures. All of it now seemed like a distant dream, drowned in the autumn rain that softly fell on the abandoned doorstep.

Autumn leaves were scattered across the yard, the light drizzle blending with the tears on little Dall's face. That grief—cold and relentless—etched itself deep into her mind, and with it grew a hatred for the dreary autumn, that quiet emptiness which took away what she loved most.

Paula's long-time "good-for-nothing boyfriend," as she used to whisper about him in secret, inherited the house after her death. For Dall and Mira, this meant only one thing—another move, another beginning in the unknown.

Mira stayed the entire summer season, while Dall returned in mid-August, as school began at the start of September. That summer, Dall was placed in the care of an elderly couple who lived near the "Stipo Đerek" elementary school, where she attended classes.

Although they pretended before Mira that they adored children, their performance was like something out of a Grimm's fairy tale—a perfect lie that concealed a harsh reality. In their home, the cold did not come only from winter. They were irritable, miserable, and stingy with affection.

Having never had children of their own, they did not know how to offer tenderness. Everything Dall did seemed to provoke their irritation, which often ended in shouting and scolding—and so Dall learned that silence could sometimes be the only refuge.

For a child who loved spending her days outside, immersed in countless activities shaped by curiosity, resources, and, of course, money—Dall had none of that here. With her small but perceptive heart, she felt the chill directed at her within those walls.

With her small but perceptive heart, she felt the cold directed at her in that house. Without a word being spoken, she knew these people did not love her, that their hearts would never warm to her. Guided by that realization, she spent most of her time in the nearby park, knowing that at home no one would miss her.

That part of town, with its tall apartment blocks, mostly belonged to intellectuals and old residents—the so-called "upper class." And precisely because of that, Dall felt like an intruder in her own world. To cope with the loneliness, she invented all sorts of games, letting her imagination run wild. She made chains from bits of twine, crafted stars, and tirelessly swung from the metal bars that once held swings—her little world of freedom.

At school, however, she was met by a teacher with many years of service, a woman of the old school—

district and often harsh. With little hesitation she punished with the cane, and pulling children's ears was her customary "disciplinary measure." She was a woman prone to prejudice.

On the very first day of school, she demanded that all children of divorced parents stand up—immediately shaming poor Dall and the handful of other pupils who found themselves in the same situation. For a six-year- old girl, the whole ordeal was deeply traumatic. Dall decided she would ignore the fuss about divorced parents, pretending to be utterly indifferent, even bored to death. Yet when someone with authority, like their teacher, deliberately singled out such things, it could not pass without consequence.

Whether she was aware of it or not, the teacher had ruined those children's reputations at the very start of their schooling. She often seized the chance to make a cruel remark about Dall's clothes, which were neither new nor fashionable, or about the lack of school supplies others took for granted—sisters to share with, stationery, everything that was readily available to the rest but not to her. Because of all this, Dall endured ridicule and teasing through her first two years of

school. Yet she never gave up. She tried hard to make a good impression, worked diligently, and strove to adapt and prove her worth. Still, the teacher saw her as lower class—a girl without a father's support and without a large family to stand behind her.

She was often reminded of her "place," made to feel different and less worthy. Dall often questioned why only her mother was in her life.

Why didn't her father fulfill his duty the way other fathers did? Why had the other relatives—those she knew existed somewhere out there—never shown the slightest desire to meet her? In those moments of loneliness, Dall stubbornly refused to let the darkness consume her. She clung tightly to the belief that one day, better, brighter times would come.

In the second grade, on the very first day of school, Dall walked in proudly dressed in brand-new, trendy clothes unlike anything her classmates had ever seen—complete with new school supplies and a shiny backpack, gifts her mother had brought. She felt their curious stares, eyes full of questions, and for once she

bloomed with joy, as though she had finally stepped out of the shadows.

Her teacher muttered under her breath, "Hm, you can tell her mother came," and continued writing on the board. People like her would never understand what it means to offer someone even a small piece of understanding, or what kind of satisfaction comes from helping another human being in any way.

The teacher often blamed Dall for things that weren't her fault—perhaps simply because there was no bond, no chemistry between them.

On one occasion, Mira was summoned to an emergency parent–teacher meeting because Dall had not followed the rules.

When the teacher asked Dall to copy the board, she could not see the faint letters and did not write. She was asked to stand in the corner as punishment but she stayed seated, and the teacher told her to go home and have her mother come because of her disrespect.

Seizing the opportunity, Mira made it clear to the schoolmistress that a person can remain true to themselves and still discipline a child using proper methods—without being an idiot. Or at the very least, find a more professional and humane way to get a seven-year-old's attention.

The teacher was undeniably shaken by this exchange, and afterward, for the most part, left Dall alone.

As time went on and Dall grew older, she realized that her teacher did not need to love her—what mattered was that she taught her what she was paid to teach. In their own way, the two learned to tolerate each other.

While Dall loved writing, reading, and poetry, she never took to the sciences. Mathematics was never her favorite subject. Luckily, she sat next to Jeca, a lively little girl always ready to play and eager to help a friend in need. Jeca's parents adored Dall, which only deepened the girls' bond.

Then there was Daniel, a boy in their class, a gifted mathematician who despised essays and writing assignments. They struck a deal: he would solve Dall's math problems, and she would help him with his literature and essays.

Both were children of single parents, and that invisible thread of shared experience created a small circle of friendship that made school days a little easier. Through those harsh eighties, Mira and Dall were more often hungry than full.

Life was hard and work increasingly scarce. For Dall, that period carried a weight of unpleasant memories, with others pushed deep into her subconscious—those painful fragments that whispered from the fog of the past.

One of the darkest demons of her childhood was tied to a visit to the village where her mother had been born. They would go to see Aunt Milica, Mira's only living relative who was still on speaking terms with her. Through the haze of memory, Dall recalled a scene in that village: a stranger on horseback rode up, leaned down, and handed out sweet candies to the children—but not to her. Trusting her instincts, Dall held herself back, ignoring the man with the same pride he showed in ignoring her.

Later, she would learn the devastating truth—that the stranger on the horse had in fact been her grandfather, Mirko. According to village gossip, Grandfather Mirko had been bitterly disappointed in Mira's choice of partner, a man who failed every one of his standards as a husband for his youngest daughter. After Mira's separation from Sajo, she had been invited back to her parents' home—on one condition: that Dall remain with her father. For unlike Mira, Dall was neither acknowledged nor welcomed as his granddaughter.

Mira refused, firmly and without hesitation. Where her child was not welcome, she would not set foot. She chose instead to remain alone with her daughter, without the support or protection of family.

Another ghost from the past lived in Dall's memory— an evening during yet another move in her second- grade year, when she and Mira went in search of a place to sleep. They knocked on the door of Mira's brother, Jovan, three years her senior, a man with whom she had once been close. Jovan was well-off, diligent, employed in a Slovenian cookware factory.

His house, where he lived with his wife, was large— but empty. For all their efforts, they had been unable to have children.

In Dall's memory, that house loomed immense and intimidating in the dusk. She hid behind her mother, anxiously awaiting who would appear at the door, feeling deep inside that she was the reason her uncle no longer spoke to his sister—that she was the unwelcome one. She could not recall the words exchanged that night, only the sorrow and pain etched on her mother's face. Dall's soul ached, powerless to help.

They continued wandering through the darkness in search of shelter, for Jovan had not allowed them to spend the night. And so, their journey went on.

That night, Dall made herself a promise: she would never again seek out so-called family. A family that brought her mother such grief was no family she would ever need. She and her mother were better off without them.

And yet—not everything was bleak. Dall held in her heart one tender memory of her grandmother Jela. She remembered the older woman who would walk for half a day from their village, just to bring them meat, cheese, eggs, or milk. She would carefully unpack the neatly wrapped goods from her woven basket, place them on the little wooden table, and urge Mira and Dall to eat...

"Come on, take some, eat a little!"

Softly, almost on tiptoe, fearing someone might see her, she would hurry back to the village before nightfall—her heart heavy, as any mothers would be. After exchanging only a few words with her daughter Mira and grand-daughter Dall, she would vanish into the night.

Dall still remembers those old, rough hands caressing her cheeks, and the tears in her grandmother's hazel- colored eyes. Then she would disappear, leaving Mira pensive and bowed, as if the weight of the entire world had settled on her shoulders. Dall, sensing her mother's silent suffering, would quietly come close and hug her without a word—sharing her burden.

Chapter 4

Through the War

Bosnia and Herzegovina, 1990's

If the 1980s had brought poverty, the 1990s brought something worse war.

"Mama, what is war?" Dall often asked, hearing that word over and over, everywhere around her. Mira tried to find the best words to explain those three letters that carried all the weight and cruelty of the world.

How could she explain that in this dreadful, abnormal state, Mira and Zada were no longer friends? That those same children might never again receive even a slice of bread from Dara? That neighbors were no longer neighbors. That children—those of mixed parentage—would carry a heavy, incomprehensible, indescribable burden?

In 1990, three major political parties were formed in Bosnia and Herzegovina.

It is significant to note that Josip Broz Tito, the president of Yugoslavia, died in May 1980, marking the end of an era in the country's history. After his death, the central authority of the League of Communists of Yugoslavia weakened, and nationalist and ethnic tensions, previously suppressed under Tito, began to rise.

During the 1980s, economic difficulties and political stagnation further weakened the communist system.

By the late 1980s, under Milošević in Serbia and reform movements elsewhere, Yugoslavia began allowing political pluralism.

Communism as a single-party system was still officially in place, but pressures from both internal dissent and the collapse of communism in Eastern Europe (1989) forced the League of Communists to allow multi-party elections.

In 1990, Bosnia and Herzegovina held its first multi-party elections, prompting ethnic communities to form parties like SDA, SDS, and HDZ BiH to ensure political representation.

In May that year, the SDA—Party of Democratic Action—was established, representing the rights of

citizens from the Muslim cultural circle. It stood for an indivisible and sovereign Bosnia and Herzegovina, led by Alija Izetbegović. Shortly afterward, the SDS— Serb Democratic Party—was founded, advocating the idea that Serbs must defend their identity. And finally, in August 1990, came the HDZ—Croatian Democratic Union—pushing either for Yugoslavia's transformation into a confederation or, failing that, for an independent Bosnia and Herzegovina.

For Dall, those childhood years were marked by fear, hunger, the struggle for survival, and an unavoidable darkness...

Mira worked in the outskirts of the town, in the district known by its postal code 70230, while Dall spent every free moment in the small town on the Vrbas River—where she felt safest, most loved, most accepted.

The changes came quietly at first. A teacher absents without explanation. A neighbor who suddenly stopped greeting them in the stairwell. Men whispering in cafés late into the night. Then came the louder signs: checkpoints on the roads, soldiers with rifles where only policemen once stood, the sound of distant gunfire echoing across the hills.

Bugojno was no longer the town Dall had first known. Streets that once bustled with children and vendors now carried an uneasy silence. Friends stopped visiting, families pulled back into their own corners, and suspicion replaced laughter in the courtyards.

At school, the divisions sharpened. Desks seemed farther apart, conversations shorter, questions sharper. Dall felt eyes on her—curious, judging, questioning. She was no longer simply the girl with two names; she had become a symbol of something children couldn't name but had already learned to fear.

"Which side are you on?" one boy demanded during recess, his voice carrying the echoes of adult arguments.

"I don't know," she whispered, but the truth was she knew there was no safe answer.

On that fateful day, Mira rushed home from work—not only to bring Dall back but also to help Ibro and his family leave their beloved home. Soldiers paraded

through the streets with rifles, barricades rose at every corner—it all foreshadowed the heavy, dark days that seemed unavoidable for everyone.

People locked themselves inside their houses. A mass exodus had begun. Dall, confused, tried to make sense of whispers about "ours," "theirs," and "mine," words adults murmured both in the street and at home.

Ibro's family temporarily settled in the tiny attic apartment where Mira and Dall lived. Safa's greatest worry was her older son, who could be mobilized at any moment, so she sent him away on the first convoy to her daughter in Austria. Safa herself, with her youngest boy, stayed for a while with Mira and Dall.

Ibro remained, a silent guardian of the home he had inherited from his father, refusing stubbornly to leave, as if the walls themselves depended on his watchful presence.

Panic reigned everywhere. Families packed their entire lives into two suitcases. Some braver souls remained behind, determined to guard their hearths. Curtains and thick blankets covered windows so that no light could slip outside— "God forbid" someone should see it. On the ground floors, sandbags lined the window frames in case of stray bullets.

For Dall, those days were a haze. All the rushing, the panic, the uncertainty—none of it made sense to her young mind.

A few days later, Safa announced she would move in with acquaintances in the nearby Gaj neighborhood, since the tiny attic was too cramped for everyone.

Later, Mira learned they had fled to Croatia—probably unwilling to be a burden—leaving without telling her or Dall.

Mira's former colleague and godmother Ljuba lived in Austria. Through years of friendship with Vedran's mother, Mira had come to know the entire family.

When Vedran was sent to Austria to be with his mother until the situation calmed—safe from mobilization—Mira and Dall were invited to move in with Luka and his wife Ruža, so they would not be alone.

Mira didn't want to face those days with just her child, nor did she wish to leave for a foreign country, so the offer seemed logical—and tempting. Yet Dall felt a sharp empathy for her mother, fearing deep down that perhaps she herself was the reason for Mira's endless troubles. The name Dall carried was unwanted among her mother's people, while Mira's name was unwanted in the place where they now lived.

Ruža and Luka, their new hosts, shared the same burden—they too were a mixed marriage—and in those years they faced similar trials and dilemmas. That thread of shared fate tied them together, and so Mira and Dall found a measure of safety in their home.

But from the streets once filled with children chasing each other through the mahala—from the cherished neighborhood where Dall grew up, where elastic games echoed, where early fruits perfumed the air, where unity and love stitched life together—there came a new time: bleak and sorrowful.

And yet, even in that settlement, there were still children.

At the top of the street lived a Czech family: father and son bore the same name, while mother and daughter both answered to Anika. The little blue-eyed Czech boy was the first to give Dall a handwritten note. She cannot recall the words, nor how that family ended up in Bugojno of all places—but she still

remembers the shaky heart drawn in pencil, with the initials P + D inside.

Nearby lived refugees from Gornji Vakuf—also known as Usko-plje—the neighboring town that was home to Sajo, Dall's father. Then there was an old Bugojno family with two sons: chubby Astor and little Darius.

In one of the houses lived a family from the nearby village of Prusac, part of Donji Vakuf municipality—a married couple with a boy and a girl. There was also a little girl named Jeni, small, with wild, untamed hair, who irresistibly resembled Pippi Longstocking. She was often found at Luka and Ruža's place, as if she were part of their large, informally bound family.

Jeni had two older brothers, Aret and Kan, and fate dealt Kan a cruel blow—at the very start of the war, he stepped on a mine and lost his leg. He was no older than twenty-two.

In the neighborhood, there were also refugees from Donji Vakuf: a family with a daughter, Diana, and a son, Samuel, who bore an uncanny resemblance to one of the members of the pop group Backstreet Boys. Samuel played football brilliantly and was a favorite among the children.

In one of the nearby houses lived a boy named Adi. His father was Albanian, and his mother suffered from mental illness. In moments without medication, she would have violent outbursts—smashing dishes and screaming, filling the house with a dreadful silence and unease. Adi would flee as soon as he sensed danger, hiding somewhere in the neighborhood, often in the abandoned houses that dotted the settlement.

Dall instinctively felt that Adi needed a friend, and she often chatted with him endlessly, inventing games and stories that would draw them closer. Play was not just children's amusement—it was survival. Jeni, chubby Astor, Adi, and Dall formed a cheerful foursome who ran through the alleys until dusk. They played hide- and-seek, built makeshift seesaws by dragging heavy wooden beams and balancing them on wooden blocks, laughing carefree despite the grim circumstances.

One Eid, in a silent gesture of gratitude, Adi brought over a plate full of baklava. He rang the bell softly, left the pastries at the door, and then ran back home as fast as his legs could carry him, afraid that someone had seen him from the windows.

Because of that gesture, Dall became the subject of teasing at school for days—but despite it, she didn't waver.

During the war, these four were the only children left in the neighborhood, and their games became their lifeline. Amid grenades and snipers, they pretended to be bulletproof, wielding imaginary superpowers as they sneaked out of their homes—remarkably, to this day, no one knows how the bullets never found them.

As the years passed, there were fewer children, and more abandoned houses.

Mira was busy cleaning, washing carpets, and taking on various jobs at Ruža's house and around the neighborhood to earn enough for a meal. It was not much, but it mattered.

Dall always had a special sensitivity for people, and she instinctively kept out of Luka's way from morning until evening, sensing that in some unspoken way, she bothered him. When Luka was sober, without "a glass too many," Dall could read the moment and join him in a game of cards or dominoes for amusement.

But when his dark moods took hold, she would escape outside, not wanting to cross his path.

Day and night she invented games with the remaining children in the neighborhood, or she would spend time at a nearby neighbor's home, seeking at least a sliver of joy in a world that often felt unbearably heavy.

Life never coddled Dall, but it was precisely that reality that taught her to cherish every moment, to find immense joy in the smallest things.

As the whispers of the remaining children in the settlement grew quieter, Dall began spending more time with the neighbors—Rada and Anton. They were another young mixed-marriage couple in the neighborhood, highly educated and, in many ways, completely out of place in the primitive environment around them. They lived together with Anton's mother, and since Anton often worked outside the home, Rada spent much of her time alone.

Anton was a quiet and reserved man, a person of few words but always busy—

whether tending his garden, riding his beloved bicycle to the market, or reading one of his favorite books. He never idled or wasted time. At first glance, he appeared restrained, almost cold—the opposite of his brother Ante, who was loud and talkative. Yet, despite rarely showing emotions, Anton was a man of kind heart, always ready to lend a hand.

A great patriot, Anton loved his Bugojno—the city where he had grown up and laid down roots, far from the turmoil of the outside world. He believed that young people should remain in the place where they were born—to study, to love, to nurture their homeland, and in return to invest all their strength and knowledge in the future of their country.

For Dall, he was a distant figure, but in a way, she became a source of diversion for Rada—his soft- spoken wife, often lonely, without any real bond with her mother-in-law, and with even less connection to women of her own age in the neighborhood.

Anton's mother, Mrs. Dunja, was a frequent guest in Luka's house. She would take a glass or two of rakija and chatter endlessly with the household.

For Dall, that was always a clear signal—it was time to slip away and go to Rada's.

Times were hard, but every new acquaintance, every new habit, carried with it a trace of progress, however small. Rada would spend hours teaching Dall how to embroider, talking with her, or simply reading. For Dall, Anton and Rada's home became a refuge—a shelter from everyday life—while for Rada, Dall was a spark of freshness, someone with whom she could share thoughts, silence, or just the passing of time.

Dall had always been an impatient, curious child, and although she had two left hands for embroidery, she tried to learn at least the simplest patterns. Not to master them, but to please Rada, who passed on her knowledge with such patience.

The true jewel of that home, however, was Anton's wall—a proper home library. From floor to ceiling, the shelves were lined with books: the collected works of Dostoevsky, Andrić, Yesenin, Tolstoy, encyclopedias, manuals, classics, and even the occasional comic. A small treasure hidden behind ordinary doors.

Dall would carefully choose her books, devour the pages by candlelight or lantern, return them to Anton, and with a sparkle in her eye retell the stories, the lessons, the characters, the authors... before eagerly reaching for the next one.

Books were her first great love. With Robinson Crusoe she survived on a deserted island, with young Werther she grieved for an unattainable love, she wandered through civilizations of mammoths, explored the world through comics, philosophy, and fantasy. Books were her weapon, her refuge, and above all—her window into a better world. It can rightly be said: books shaped her view of life.

Dall adored this new, undiscovered world of books—a marvelous realm of characters and adventures that carried her far away from harsh reality, above the sounds of sirens, the whispers of mobilization, and the anxiety of days filled with dread. Books took her where she was allowed to be a child.

On many occasions, Anton and Rada—gentle but quiet anchors of her childhood—fed her, though Dall never asked for anything. She came with an empty stomach, modestly, not wanting to be a burden, but their doors and hearts were always open. This young couple helped both Mira and Dall, then and much later—when the war fell silent, but all the other wounds kept bleeding.

Dall admired Rada's talent, wondering where all that imagination came from, all that beauty woven into the embroidered tablecloths that adorned the table in their apartment. Rada's taste was refined, unobtrusive, and every detail in their home bore the stamp of attention and love.

Anton's apartment was on the second floor of the house, and its ambiance, style, peace, and intellectual silence made it a small sanctuary in a world that was collapsing. Their little courtyard was always neat, and the tidy rows of flowers and the scent of raspberries lingered with Dall like traces of sunlight. The sweet raspberries she would secretly pick on her way out were like a reward for a child who had to grow up far too quickly.

In the whirlwind of life, one quiet morning, Rada discovered she was carrying a child. Dall was overjoyed. She celebrated each step of the pregnancy, hoping she could help, that she could be useful. That she might even have the honor of helping with the baby—little Lakas—whose name she pronounced with awe. A year later, another gift arrived in the same home—Viorko.

It was then that Dall, slowly and quietly, began to withdraw. She sensed that this young family now needed peace, privacy, space to grow, to bond, to breathe as one. She stepped back without noise, but with deep love, knowing that Anton and Rada had given her more than food, books, and attention. They had given her a model of what peace looked like.

Love. Respect.

In her heart, she kept their home as one of the rare safe harbors of her childhood. Whatever else the years had taken from her, the time she spent with Anton and Rada she never forgot. It was thanks to those young, quiet, yet great people that the years of darkness and pain became, if only slightly, more bearable.

A glimmer of light in a time when darkness had become everyday life. On the other side, however, inside Ružica and Luka's house, the situation was growing heavier with each passing day. The constant stress, the uncertainty, and the weight everyone carried pressed down on Luka.

His temperament, fragile and frayed under the burden of war and alcohol, grew more unpredictable.

It was then that Luka's brother, Nenad, in one of his darkest moments, revealed a plan of escape—an improvised attempt to cross the front lines, following a route he hoped would take them to Croatia and from there... anywhere that would open its doors. The plan was reckless, risky, and barely thought through. A small group of people decided to try.

At first, Mira, exhausted and worn down by the daily struggle, agreed. She sat Dall down, explained everything to her, sternly, seriously, as she never had before:

"When we start, you don't stop. No: I'm hungry, I'm thirsty, I can't go on. You just walk, stay quiet, keep moving. Until we reach safety. No fear. No questions."

Dall, still a child, listened wide-eyed, holding her breath—sensing that something great and dangerous was about to happen. But at the very last moment, Mira pulled back. A mother's heart overpowered the despair of a woman. Her fear for Dall was greater than hunger, winter, or grenades combined. She feared losing the only thing she had—and chose not to go. To stay.

A few days later the news arrived. The group had stumbled into a minefield. Nenad had lost a leg. Several others were wounded. Many barely made it out alive. That night, Mira wept quietly. In her heart, for the hundredth time, she thanked God for the decision to stay. For keeping her little girl safe. From that day forward, no such attempts ever crossed her mind again. The price was too high. And she realized—even freedom is worthless if you have no one to share it with.

Not long after, the house where Mira and Dall were staying was looted. Masked soldiers stormed Luka's home, leaving behind chaos, fear, and an even deeper sense of insecurity. After that, Luka grew paranoid, irritable, and nearly unbearable to live with.

Dall, whether she wanted to or not, overheard the hushed conversations of the adults, whispered in corners of the house, conversations that never held anything good for her or Mira. She knew—they were no longer welcome, that they were in the way.

To avoid being a burden, she stayed outside as much as she could, spending her days in the company of Luka's hunting dog—a black-and-white greyhound named Linda. She grew so attached to that quiet, faithful companion that she would share even the last bite of canned meat from her lunch with her. Linda followed her everywhere, as if she too felt Dall's sadness and loneliness, asking nothing in return— except to be nearby.

Luka no longer hid his dissatisfaction with having Mira and her daughter under his roof. More often, and more openly, he said it was time for them to leave to "find their own way."

And in those days, when it seemed, they had nowhere left to turn, as if conjured from the ground itself, appeared the infamous figure of Dall's father. From nowhere—never truly present, yet suddenly there—he managed to persuade the owner of the small flat where they once lived to take them back in.

It was a new chapter. Not an easy one, not a happy one, but theirs.

By then, Dall had already learned to keep her emotions under control. In front of her mother, she hid every trace of fear, every shiver of anxiety in her chest—wanting to spare her any more tears.

She grew up too soon, in silence. They moved into an old attic flat—small, but familiar. Beneath them, on the ground floor, lived the family who owned the house. They had two children: a daughter, Sana, a few years older than Dall, and a son, Ari, a year or two younger. It was a modest home, without luxury, but it was theirs. After everything, it felt as if they once again had a corner of the world, they could call their own.

Although tensions over religious belonging did not fade, in time all the tenants of the house learned to endure, and even to quietly respect one another. Life, however cruel, forced people to find a common language—even if only through the routines of everyday survival.

Adem's daughter, already in her teenage years, wore what were then considered stylish "shop" hairstyles— teased, lacquered, with strands curling around her face like draped curtains. Dall admired her boldness, her poise, and her look, which seemed to her like glamour straight out of foreign films. Ari, her younger brother, was a quiet child. Withdrawn, shy, struggling in school—especially with English and mathematics.

As the war raged beyond their walls and hunger gnawed at them, Dall understood she could help Ari—and maybe, just maybe, offer a morsel of relief to her and her mother at last.t his mother's request, Dall began tutoring Ari.

She taught him patiently and gently, not for money, but out of a sense that it was simply the right thing to do. Still, those lessons often brought food to their table—a sack of flour, a carton of eggs, half a loaf of bread. In those days, that was wealth.

Adem—stern and reserved on the surface—was an honest man. Though many in the neighborhood whispered behind his back, "How can you keep them—those others—in your house, in times like these?" he had a way of silencing them all. He looked at people, not at surnames. Mira was grateful, though never servile. Dall, even as a child, recognized this— and respected him in silence, as one respect the rare, brave few who ask for nothing in return.

Despite everything—the shells falling as if to scorch away every trace of childhood, the "zvončići," (cluster bomblets that looked like toys but exploded at the slightest touch) "krmače," (massive aerial bombs locals grimly nicknamed "sows") and other deadly weapons whose names children memorized before the names of flowers—Dall was a diligent student. An honor pupil. Classes were held wherever possible—in basements, checkpoints, shelters—and always interrupted. If they managed three days of school in a row, it was considered a success. But Dall never gave up. Knowledge was her only certain ticket to a better future.

The way she grew up—between ruins, ideological borders, and invisible walls—left an indelible mark. The years of darkness, fear, and survival made her both fragile and unbreakably strong. She learned to see herself at both extremes—at her worst, and at her very best.

She hated everything that divided people. Religious, ethnic, social barriers all seemed meaningless to her— for she knew, firsthand, how much pain and destruction could come from the idea that you must belong to something simply because you were told to.

She longed for peace—not the political kind, but a personal one, the quiet peace where people could simply be who they are. And for that silence, she was ready to give everything. What could happen to her—had already happened.

From the years spent in basements while grenades tore the sky, through the daily struggle for a meal, to the deeper, suffocating distrust of people that life's circumstances taught her. Yet, despite it all, Dall never lost faith in one thing—knowledge.

She believed in the world of books. She believed there had to be something better. Somewhere out there, beyond trenches and borders, there was a world where people were not shot for their surnames or hated for their names. In those books she found such worlds.

Every page was a window—into the past, the future, into the possible and the impossible. She saw them as humanity's most beautiful achievement—dreams written by hand, captured thoughts, cries, hopes, and premonitions poured into words. Books taught her to think, to doubt, to question. To dream.

Thanks to Anton—his library, his trust, his silence, his presence—Dall found the most important thing: a bond with reading, with learning, with herself.

Mira was a devoted mother—but when it came to school, Dall was left to herself. Not because Mira didn't want to help, but because she couldn't.

Exhausted from days filled with struggle, physical work, and injustice, Mira didn't have the strength to wrestle with books and lessons. But she believed in Dall—and that was enough.

Dall grew through that belief. Alone, but never lost. Driven by an inner need to survive—not only with her body, but with her spirit. That later proved to be an advantage, though at the time it may have felt like a burden. Many parents, wanting to help, take on their children's tasks, writing homework instead of them and unknowingly robbing them of the chance to develop critical thinking, independence, and work habits. Dall never had that "luxury." Her homework was hers alone.

From early childhood she learned to find solutions on her own, to explore, to make mistakes and try again. And although Mira, like any mother, carried that inborn fear for her child, she also had what mattered most—a sense of measure. She instinctively understood that Dall had to learn on her own, because that was the only way she would succeed.

The school system, like so many others, tried to fit children into predetermined boxes—but Dall did not always fit. Children's maturity cannot always be measured by the same scale, nor are difficulties always visible.

One day, Mira tried to help Dall with math. They sat at the table, pencils and notebooks ready, but the material was difficult, tangled, full of gaps. Mira grew impatient, frustrated, and Dall felt the tightening grip of not knowing. She felt stupid, helpless—and worst of all was watching her mother lose patience.

That day Dall made an important, and sad, decision: she would no longer ask for help.

"I'll manage," she told herself in silence. "I'll ask someone from class, study again, somehow, I'll understand."

She didn't want her mother upset. She didn't want their little time together wasted on anger and disappointment. She wanted that precious time tied to laughter, hugs, and tenderness—not to numbers that brought tears.

In that way, without even realizing it, she took another step closer to independence—quietly, unobtrusively, as she always did.

Dall managed as best as she knew how. She showed good results at school, though little escaped her mother's watchful eye. Mira was strict about keeping Dall's grades at the expected level.

"You must study, so you don't end up being everyone's broom and shovel, like me," she often said, looking at her with a mix of sternness and love.

"Not to be in vain."

Those words carved themselves into Dall like a vow. They guided her in every future decision, like a compass cutting through fog. Each time she paused, each time she doubted, she would recall her mother's sacrifice—and keep moving forward.

She dreamed of a different life. A life without chains and fears, without war and grenades, without brainwashing through foreign ideologies and suffocating rules. She never again wanted to be shoved into a box—by faith, by origin, by name. She imagined that one day her children would never have to choose which side they belonged to. That they would be free to be—only themselves. That they would be defined by character, effort, and achievement, not by surname, party, or their parents' position.

While war still raged outside and grenades fell on the nearby hills, Dall looked toward the sky, praying that one day all of it would be nothing more than a distant past—not only for her mother, but even more so for herself.

Mira, on the other hand, stood firmly on the ground. She did not drift into clouds like Dall. She was a woman of experience, not imagination. The years had taught her caution and persistence. Through all those bleak days, she built unbreakable friendships with neighboring refugees, women much like her. With honesty, hard work, and an unshakable character, Mira earned respect—and with it, doors opened to her when no one else had the key.

Strong and unwavering, Mira was, to Dall, the embodiment of everything she herself was not yet— everything she lacked: strength, confidence, peace within resolve. Mira never faltered. Each day she rose anew, as if the previous one had never even happened.

From the depth of her own pain, Mira drew strength for each new day, for that "better tomorrow" she so firmly believed was waiting for her and her daughter.

Dall, on the other hand, remembered every detail—the silence of basements, the smell of damp walls and candles, the fear that settled like a heavy blanket as soon as the sun went down. All those war hardships she would carry with her forever—as indelible marks on her soul.

She was in the fifth grade when they moved to the neighborhood near the department store Talijanka. And even in those years of darkness, children still found ways to gather, to share the little they had—a piece of bread, a handkerchief, a smile—and to try, through play, to forget reality.

At the very beginning of the street lived a family with two children, and their son, Marius, was Dall's age.

Next to their house stood the home of the well-known town doctor, Mr. Rujanac, with his wife and son.

Across the way was the house where Zlaja and his sister Maja lived children whose fathers had been mobilized into the Territorial Defense, absent somewhere on the shifting front lines, moving day by day, shell by shell. The mothers remained at home, managing however they could. They were the quiet heroines—without weapons, but with a thousand ways to fight off hunger and despair.

On that fateful day, Marius invited us to play hide- and-seek in one of the many abandoned houses. It was an unusually calm day—no grenades, no sirens, not a single shot. Peace, so rare in those times, encouraged the children to, if only for a moment, forget reality.

We ran breathlessly, made slingshots out of broken wires, and laughter flew across our faces as if we were not living in the middle of a war.

Marius's mother handed out wild, tiny apples to the children—sour, hard, but in that moment the sweetest fruit Dall's lips had ever touched. Toward evening, everyone headed home, while Marius, flushed with excitement, ran to see his father who had just returned from the front.

A few hours later, Dall remembered the screams—not human, but more like animal cries. Long, painful, piercing. They came from Marius's house and tore through the night. People poured out of their homes, trying to understand what had happened. Children were pulled away from windows, forbidden to step outside. That night, Dall curled against Mira, tightly, like a lost kitten. She did not sleep—she only waited for the night to end.

By morning, the news spread through the neighborhood like poisoned breath. Marius's father, exhausted and worn, had left his pistol—loaded—in a drawer. While he showered, Marius, playing, found the weapon. And in that child's game—that should never have existed—a shot rang out. The boy had accidentally killed himself.

If human life is woven of both joy and sorrow, and often unpredictable, it was confirmed in the story of this eleven-year-old boy's family. No collection of words could even remotely capture the grief of his mother for her only child. Dark, heavy grief covered the neighborhood, the green lawns, and the hearts of Marius's little group of friends, leaving behind eternal scars.

A week later, though Dall tried with all her might to avoid the house where Marius had lost his life, his mother called his small group of friends. In her hands, she carried a handful of apples—not the tart ones they had once loved so much, especially Dall, but bitter ones, as bitter as the grief in her eyes, where all the sorrow of the world could be read and seen.

Softly, almost in a whisper, she said that Marius would surely want his friends to have those apples, even if he was no longer there to share them himself— and that she wanted the tradition to live on.

Never again in her life did Dall long for wild apples. They left a lasting, bitter taste on her lips, never again to remind her of childhood—because playful Marius, with sparks of joy in his eyes, was gone forever.

In all that turmoil, Dall's concentration faltered—she began to seriously fall behind in math. The material piled up, and she understood less and less. The math teacher of that time gave priority to students who brought him boxes of tobacco or comic books like Zagor, Captain Miki, Alan Ford, and the like.

While some classmates came with large blue boxes of tobacco, Dall was a collector of comics, and she decided to part with her beloved collection so she wouldn't face problems with a teacher who often smelled of alcohol.

The solution presented itself when Mira announced that her colleague—an aunt of Dall's childhood friends—was coming to visit. Aunt Ajla, though she sometimes smelled of alcohol, was extremely intelligent and an outstanding mathematician. Her visits became increasingly frequent, almost as if Aunt Ajla had in some way moved in with Mira and Dall.

Ajla's family had fled to Austria, and apart from her younger sister and elderly mother, she was alone. The days spent with Aunt Ajla bore fruit, because Mira— direct and decisive as ever—insisted that Aunt Ajla train Dall in everything she was lagging behind in for math.

Day after day, Dall worked diligently with Aunt Ajla, and the essential, much-needed mathematical foundation she acquired was the result of that bond. Mutual—because Aunt Ajla, often absent from her own family's home, seemed to find a kind of family in them too.

Dall remembers that her father came from time to time, sometimes bringing Mira a pack of cigarettes, a wafer, or some other small token of attention for Dall. She delighted in those visits, strutting proudly like a peacock, eager for everyone to see and hear that she, too, had a father—that he was there.

Unfortunately, Aunt Ajla seemed to enjoy one of those visits a little too much, with a glass of rakija in hand, and it brought nothing good. After that, she stopped coming to Mira and Dall's home.

Dall assumed Mira wanted her to stay away because of a little too much drinking, or Aunt Ajla decided so—whatever it was, the visits ended.

After the tragedy with Marius, and with her days filled with constant math drills that kept her from roaming outside, the little neighborhood gang began gathering less and less. When she could steal the time—on days when the smell of gunpowder was not so heavy in the air—she would dash across the street to trade napkins with Zlaja's sister.

Dall kept her napkins and chocolate wrappers in a blue tobacco tin. Zlaja was two years older than she was, a handsome teenager, while Maja was a small, freckled redheaded girl, forever pouting, who irresistibly reminded Dall of the old children's rhyme "Srda" by Jovan Jovanović Zmaj. Dall never held Maja's sulking against her, and the two would spend hours sitting on the doorstep of their house, swapping napkins and marveling at chocolate wrappers, discussing which ones they had tasted and which they longed to try.

They were happy with such little things, forgetting how long it had been since they'd tasted chocolate.

If they ate anything other than lentils or beans, it was already reason enough for a lively debate. While the adults' biggest obstacles were the lack of electricity, water, and telecommunication, Dall had adapted to the conditions as if they were perfectly normal, making the most of daylight before the curfew came, when everyone had to be indoors.

During the summer holidays she spent her days wandering the empty streets, climbing over fences, exploring abandoned houses, or keeping Maja company when she could. Mira scolded her 11 years old child daily, yelling that she didn't want her leaving the yard, but the little rebel with a restless spirit that Dall was always found a way to sneak out and begin a new adventure.

When the weather was bad, or her mood matched it, Dall shortened the days with books—her endless love. She adored fantasy, though Mira often scolded her for living in the clouds and would frequently check what Dall was reading. That's how it was with parents, Dall thought as she lay awake under the small kerosene lamp: it wasn't good if you read, and it wasn't good if you didn't. Mira would grumble that she would ruin her eyes and that it was time to sleep.

Dall never liked sharing her great love for books with her peers. She often met with misunderstanding or mockery, being told she was wasting her time fantasizing, that such books were stupid and pointless. That infuriated her—because, in her mind, someone had to imagine and shape an entire world that didn't exist, and surely that could not have been easy.

So, while other children were punished with the words, "Go to your room and read," for Dall the harshest punishment was hearing, "Put that book down and go outside."

Toward the end of summer vacation, Dall came down with chicken-pox. Feverish and miserable, she thought that every bad thing that could happen seemed to choose her. Not long before, she had suffered a terrible toothache, and they had taken her to one of the so-called dentists—Asim, a man known in the village for doing dental work at home. Under the influence of alcohol, Asim pulled the wrong tooth while Dall sat on a small wooden bench in his house. After dealing with that entire tooth drama—pain, infection, swelling, and sleepless nights—she finally began to recover. A few days later, red spots began appearing on her stomach and soon spread across her entire body. Dall was beside herself with anger, especially when she heard that the few children left in the neighborhood had been invited across the street, to Majda and Zlaja's, for his birthday party. Through tears, she begged her mother to let her go, imagining a lavishly decorated room and all the treats she would miss.

But Mira was firm in her decision—Dall could not go outside. She listed her reasons one by one: chickenpox was contagious, it could leave permanent scars if not taken care of properly, and she patiently explained that Dall surely didn't want to infect the whole street. She needed rest. Dall's pleading had no effect—she was furious with her mother.

That afternoon, the air raid sirens wailed, and soon the shells began to fall. It had become normal—people were so accustomed to the sound of sirens, bullets, and grenades that, unless one struck near their home, the deafening noise was just part of daily life. Dall remembers how the temperature in the room seemed to shift, how the plates on the table jumped on their own, as if their little attic apartment had been overtaken by ghosts.

Adem called to Mira and Dall from halfway down the stairs, shouting at them not to "fool around" and to get down to the school basement immediately, because this was not a good sign.

They ran down the steps as if chased by death itself. A shell fell so close that no one could tell whether it had struck their house or the one next door.

Fear gripped everyone; no one dared open the doors. Huddled together in the basement, they waited for the shelling to stop.

The shells fell like rain—into courtyards, onto streets—explosions echoing from every direction, roofs collapsing under the impact. Each person was trapped in their own thoughts, some whispering prayers, but all of them sharing the same realization: if this passes us by, it's nothing less than a miracle, a lottery win. It was one of those moments when a person asks: what is the point of my existence? Why am I here? Where will I go after this?

This wasn't the first shelling, nor would it be the last. Shells fell almost daily, but people adapted, numbed themselves to the sounds, learning to live with the unbearable.

When the coalition known as the Territorial Defense collapsed and clashes broke out between Muslims and Croats—while battles with the Army of the Serbian Republic still raged—the situation for the remaining civilians grew even worse.

It was a sweltering July of 1993, oppressive in a way that defied explanation. New refugees poured into the neighborhood while the city's residents streamed out. In July 1993, after the political split between the Croatian Community of Herceg-Bosna and the governing bodies of the Republic of Bosnia and Herzegovina, open conflict broke out in the town that—during Austro-Hungarian rule—is believed to have borne the name Wugein. Fighting erupted between the Croatian Defence Council, the HVO, and the Army of the Republic of Bosnia and Herzegovina, the ARBiH. By early August, most of the HVO had withdrawn from the municipality, yet the war across the former Yugoslavia showed no signs of relenting.

When the terrible sounds of the shelling finally died away, and everyone realized the immediate danger had passed, they rushed upstairs to see what damage had been done. Adem's house, by sheer luck, had not been hit—which could only mean one thing: one of the immediate neighbors surely had.

Together, they all spilled out into the street. Dust and thick smoke hung everywhere; the air choked with the stench of gunpowder. Dall, her ears still ringing from the endless blasts, couldn't make sense of what was happening. The earth in the yard was torn apart, uneven, scattered. Mira gripped Dall's hand tightly, gesturing that she must not touch anything—a child is a child—quick to reach for a shard of metal, a fragment of a shell, or some other deadly remnant—and in an instant, tragedy could strike. This time, Dall was utterly terrified. Neither chickenpox nor her anger at her mother mattered anymore—only the raw, primal fight for survival.

She drowned in a storm of feelings—fear, gratitude, and immeasurable relief. If there was a higher power, Dall was certain it had heard the one plea of her heart: not to take away the only thing she had in the world— her mother. She didn't worry for herself. Every fiber of her being trembled only at the thought that something might happen to Mira.

When the shelling finally fell silent, through the thick smoke and the eerie hush came faint, agonized sobs from the direction of Maja's house. Mira, her voice sharp and commanding, ordered Dall to go back inside—shouting that she belonged in bed, not wandering the street. But Dall sensed something terrible had happened. She knew her mother was

trying to shield her from the "unseen," from whatever horror had just unfolded.

Neighbors gathered in a circle, peering through the haze, but nothing was clear. Dall retreated to her room and closed her eyes.

Zlaja—the blond-haired, thirteen-year-old boy—was dead. On his birthday. A shell, a "ground-to-ground," had fallen into his yard. Curious, the teenager had hurried toward the small basement passage to see what had happened—just as a stray piece of shrapnel pierced him straight through the heart.

Zlaja would never finish school. He would never taste the sweetness of first love, nor the joy of family life. A boy still growing, gentle, good, beloved by all—his right to live, to dream, to have a future, was ripped away.

His mother watered the torn-up earth with her tears, her cries wrenching the night as she called out for her only son. She never recovered from the loss. For days she sat on the porch, motionless, as if waiting for Zlaja to come back. She barely spoke anymore. Only her eyes spoke—sometimes glimmering in rare moments of presence, perhaps when a memory of her son lit up her soul.

Dall cried for days, cursing the war and all who had caused it. She could not understand how anyone could be indifferent to such loss. How could the world not see, not hear—those cries, that pain, that devastation?

Soon after, Dall realized she was no longer welcome in Maja's house. She had become one of "the others," one of "them," the reason—so they said—that Maja was left without her brother. Dall didn't know why—whether it was shame, grief, or just unbearable sorrow—but she stopped trying.

The street lost its children's laughter. Refugees came and went, faces passing through like shadows. Dall no longer wanted to meet anyone new. She couldn't bear the thought of another loss.

Most of the time, she was alone studying, reading, sometimes spending time with Adem's children. Life, cruel as it was, went on. With the new school year and new duties, everyone turned inward, back to their own survival.

Sixth grade was better. Classes were still often interrupted by air raid sirens, but Dall had learned to live with the unpredictability of war. And though she still hated mathematics, she unexpectedly fell in love with physics. Communicating vessels, pressure, quantum and optical physics—all fed her insatiable curiosity.

Her teacher, a Montenegrin named Drago, was nearly two meters tall, with a broad smile—and, most importantly for Dall, he was the best teacher she had ever had. Patient, unconditionally so. As the Americans would say—completely "laid back." He paid little attention to the snide remarks about his religion or origins.

It turned out he, too, was in a mixed marriage. With his wife, Almasa, a biology professor, he shared the same hardships: insults, threats, and the daily weight of constant pressure.

They had no children, but in a way, Drago seemed to find a fatherly bond with Dall. He sympathized with her. And he always pushed her—forward, further, higher. At times Dall would protest, pretending to be annoyed, but deep down she loved the challenges. She loved the chance to prove that she could do it—and that his faith in her was not in vain.

Dall had a special bond with her English teacher. She adored her—quietly, sincerely, without reserve.

Miska, on the other hand, valued effort above all and recognized in Dall something beyond the average student. Dall had been learning English since the fourth grade, and any book she could find in that language—provided it was simple enough to understand—she devoured. She desperately wanted to master a foreign language. She had a natural talent for languages, and learning English came to her easily, almost instinctively. As simple as beans, Mira would say, quoting a folk phrase.

Her other, unfulfilled dream was to play a musical instrument. She had a keen sense of rhythm, loved music with all her being, but had no means to nurture it—no instruments, no lessons, no opportunities.

Teacher Miska often asked her to help younger students with basic expressions and dialogues. As the only foreign language teacher in the school, Miska simply couldn't manage everything alone. Dall felt useful, important—and perhaps more than anything, that gave her a sense of belonging.

During the war years, Dall also wrote poetry. Quietly, secretly. She never liked anyone to read it. It was hers. Too personal, too intimate to be shared with the outside world. But it was her great, quiet passion— words that could not be spoken found their refuge on paper. She loved essays, language, and literature— always excelling in them.

Toward the end of sixth grade, the students received unexpected news: a small group of selected children would have the chance to travel to Norway—for a short respite, a gift from kind people abroad. Teacher Miska didn't hesitate. She immediately nominated Dall. She fit every criterion: a child of a single mother, from a mixed marriage, with knowledge of the language, and an excellent student. After much hesitation, countless conversations, promises, and questions, the decision was finally made—and overjoyed, Dall's name was on the list.

It was a light in the middle of darkness.

As Dall nervously prepared for her first great journey, Mira, with difficulty and love, tried to gather a few pieces of clothing to outfit her decently. A bit here, a donation there, something someone had given—all for that one purpose: that her child would travel to a faraway, safe land. When all the papers had been submitted, only one signature was missing—Dall's father, Sajo, had to sign his consent for the child to leave the country.

The children, on edge, counted down the days until the end of the school year. It was a dream trip. A ray of sun and hope in the middle of wartime darkness.

Already on the bus, Dall befriended the program sponsors. Speaking English, she was one of the rare few who could communicate with the Norwegians and translate wherever needed. On the long journey, they were joined by a group of children from Lovren, Croatia—orphans from a children's home. Dall made every effort to be kind and gentle with them, aware of how much they lacked parental love and care.

And then—Norway. The land of dreams. The land of fairy tales. Extraordinary natural beauty, peaceful fjords, order, wealth, and tranquility. The people seemed happy—smiling, quiet, polite. And everything was so different: wooden houses painted in bright colors, like illustrations in children's picture books. In contrast to the grayness, concrete, and dust of her homeland—here everything seemed warm, colorful, like a story out of the Brothers Grimm.

Dall was placed with the family of Mr. Lars Meling, together with a boy named Vedo, a year younger than her. Vedo was quiet, reserved, well-mannered. He played the accordion. Unlike most boys her age, Dall did not find him annoying or irritating—on the contrary, she enjoyed his company. She helped him with English, and soon both blended into the daily life of the Meling family, who already had three children.

The Norwegians took them shopping, prepared unusual, sweet-and-salty dishes from their cuisine— rich with seafood and fish.

Their children spent much of their time outdoors, and from an early age, independence was expected. Unlike mothers in the Balkans, who kept their children under glass bells of protection, Norwegian mothers raised their children with freedom, responsibility, and mutual respect.

Every child had their tasks: whether it was washing dishes, hanging laundry, or tidying the yard— everything was done together. The mother was the main figure in the kitchen, but the rest of the family did not stand aside. Dall admired this system.

Everything was simple, logical, warm, and human.

In contrast, back home, it was still believed that a woman had to do everything herself—serve her husband's family, cook, wash, and remain silent.

She loved the Meling family with all her heart. They were bright, lively, organized. Always doing something, always together. The eldest son, Lars, was Dall's age. His job was to collect cans and deliver local newspapers by bicycle around the neighborhood. Dall found it fascinating. She borrowed one of the family's bicycles and joined Lars on his little "mission." They raced wildly through winding streets, competed, laughed, and came home exhausted and overjoyed. They earned their first pocket money together—and carefully counted and split it in half.

Norway was a cold country, not only in climate but in people too—somewhat restrained, reserved. But what

Dall experienced as their kindness and clarity in family relationships, to them was entirely normal. They, in turn, admired Dall's honesty, her openness, the way she shared emotions so directly, speaking with her heart and her eyes. She became like one of their own children. In a few serious conversations, they even mentioned the possibility of Dall staying with them—at least until the war was over.

One rainy morning, while Lars and Dall, as they did every day, raced down a gentle slope on their bicycles, the slick slide of wet asphalt dictated a different script. They didn't even have time to warn each other—the crash was sudden, swift, painful. Lars managed to land on his feet, but Dall flew over the handlebars, hitting the ground hard. She landed on her arm, which broke with a sickening crack. The pain was sharp, but the fear was sharper still.

In the hospital, as doctors spoke in a language she didn't understand, the adults' faces around her grew serious. Finally, a translator confirmed what she had secretly feared—the arm was broken in such a way that surgery would be necessary.

Dall turned white as the sheets on the hospital bed. She felt her heart pounding faster and faster, as if it would burst out of her chest. She wasn't so much afraid of the operation itself as of having "ruined something," of having caused a problem, of becoming a burden. Above all, she longed desperately for her mother. She knew Mira would have immediately taken charge, questioned the doctors, demanded a second opinion, and—most importantly—held her hand as they gave her anesthesia.

But Mira was not there. And Dall did not want her to know.

"No. Do not call her. Please. Don't tell her anything." She said it quietly, but firmly.

Although still just a girl, her tone carried such weight that even the adults fell silent and simply nodded. "She already has enough worries. She does not need this on top of everything."

The program sponsors, who remembered her from the bus as a chatty, curious girl with English better than half of them, came to visit. They brought flowers and an English book—about a boy who survived a shipwreck and lived on a deserted island. Through her pain, Dall gave a sly smile:

"A story about me—just without the sea."

They were gentle with her, respectful, and never once betrayed her wish that her mother is not told. They honored the fact that a twelve-year-old child was showing more responsibility and empathy than many adults.

The surgery went well. Her arm was in a cast, but her heart was still knotted with unease. When she returned to the Meling home, the children greeted her with drawings, written notes, even cakes they had baked themselves.

Lars felt guilty, though Dall never allowed him to shoulder the blame.

"Well, if nothing else, now I have a war wound from Norway," she joked, though she knew full well that some wounds were invisible.

In those moments, Dall realized just how much she missed her mother—her love, her care, her warm, maternal hands. Nostalgia would strike her like a sudden fever. On many evenings, when the night still refused to fall and she could not sleep because she was not used to such brightness, she prayed that her mother, wherever she was, would not go to bed hungry.

For the rest of her stay, Dall wore the cast, while everyone around her took strict care that she would not get hurt again. Upon her return, they filled her suitcases with gifts, and there were tears when it was time to part—promises that they would meet again.

Back in Bosnia, a storm of emotions swept over Dall. Mira looked smaller, thinner than ever before. Dall, sweating in a denim jacket in forty-degree heat, hurried to hide her arm in its cast. Mira studied her closely, curious, but decided not to press. She scolded her that evening for carelessness and mischief, for the broken arm—but behind it all was deep maternal pride as she listened to how her little girl had managed, on her own, in a faraway land among strangers for a whole month.

Dall, radiant with excitement, recounted the events of Norway again and again late into the night. And that evening, mother, and daughter fell into the deepest sleep—Dall happy and content at last in her mother's arms, and Mira holding her tight, as if to keep her from slipping away again in her dreams.

Chapter 5

Borrowed Peace

Haugesund, Norway,1994

That autumn, a family moved into the house next to Adem's. They had come from the town famous as the seat of AVNOJ (Anti-Fascist Council for the National Liberation of Yugoslavia.). Mira quickly found common ground with their daughter, Mia.

Mia's father was a forester—so much so that everyone simply called him Šumar, the Forester. Dall was certain no one ever actually learned his real name.

Their mother was a homemaker, a woman from the countryside who tended to the household. Mia worked alongside Mira, taking whatever jobs came their way—scrubbing carpets, whitewashing houses, cleaning for neighbors who needed help. Mira became both a mentor and a figure Mia could lean on.

At that time, questions of sexuality or puberty were "taboo" topics, and Mia never felt free to discuss them with her own mother. Much had changed in the way of life, but many things—especially of that kind—remained the same. On the Balkans, life was lived according to social prescriptions and expectations: it

was important to work, to be educated, to save for hard times, to start a family, to have children—and every personal choice had to be shaped around those programmed rules. You kept quiet before your elders. You kept quiet about unnecessary questions. You kept quiet when you needed advice about being ready to enter a sexual relationship. You kept quiet when your body began to change with puberty.

Mia had Mira to talk to about such things, and Mira, in turn, realized that one day she would have to talk openly with Dall about everything, when the time came. Luckily, Dall showed no signs of puberty yet, and at least that was one worry Mira did not have.

Mia also had an older brother—an eccentric character, not especially sociable or hardworking, but respectful, nonetheless. By then he was already in his mature years, while Dall was still just a brat, sometimes getting on his nerves as she wandered around their house.

The younger brother was his complete opposite. Fare was cheerful, full of energy, a hardworking teenager who helped his parents whenever he could. Fare and

Dall were often tasked with collecting aid from Caritas, Dobrotvor, or Merhamet—depending not so much on need but on which box you were sorted into based on your name and religious affiliation. They would receive a quarter of a liter of oil, a kilogram of sugar, flour, and whatever else had not been stolen by the employees of those charitable organizations.

Fare would put Dall into a wheelbarrow—the same kind used for hauling mortar or potatoes—and race with her to pick up supplies. They would return with their cart loaded, their stomachs mostly empty, but with the hope that at least that day they might have something decent to eat.

As the war dragged on, hunger grew sharper. One rainy evening, a stranger knocked quietly on Adem's door. Everyone watched him with suspicion, but after a short exchange of who he was and where he had come from, they learned that the man had walked for days, just to find a piece of bread—or anything at all to bring back to his children. Bloodied and exhausted, he poured out his hardships while Adem, with quiet dignity, handed him a head of cabbage and what little they could spare. By the next morning, he was gone.

At school that day, Dall received news that rekindled a flicker of hope. That summer, children once again had the chance to travel to Norway. A new group was being selected, and the Meling family insisted firmly that Dall must be among those chosen.

This time, however, the organization was far less polished. The children were placed in a camp with minimal conditions, sharing communal dining and recreation spaces, sleeping in cramped rooms. The camp lay about an hour and a half's drive from the small town of Haugesund, where the Meling family lived. Yet every day they would drive to pick up Dall, spend the day with her, and return her to the camp by evening.

The difference from her first trip was stark. Conditions were harsh, and the other children in the group weren't particularly kind toward her. They envied the attention she received and accused her of shirking her camp duties. Still, Dall felt deeply grateful for the Meling family's care. She accepted the chores given to her quietly, even though she did not quite understand why she had to scrub dining halls and wash dishes when she was away most of the day.

She explained honestly to the Meling's why she could not stay with them until the war was over. She knew it would break her mother's heart to leave her behind— for Mira had sacrificed everything, stripping her life bare to ensure her daughter's safety and happiness. To stay in Norway would have been, in Dall's eyes, selfish and ungrateful. More than that, she simply could not imagine life without her mother's nearness.

Fate would bring what it would, but Dall was resolute: she would return to her homeland, with all its pain and its fragile hopes.

She remembered vividly the days when Mia would knock on their door, asking Mira for a small cup of oil, or when Mira would send her over to Mia's family to borrow a few spoons of salt or a piece of bread.

Those small, seemingly trivial exchanges carried immense value in times when every bit of food was precious, and solidarity was the only force that gave people the strength to endure another day.

Ironically, despite coming from different towns and villages, despite belonging to different religions and faiths, despite the shells raining mercilessly upon them

and the dark cloud of hatred and expulsion plans looming over their lives, people still shared the little they had. They split the last piece of bread, a handful of flour, a few potatoes—whatever they could scavenge—knowing that only together could they survive.

Dall often recalled that unusual inner calm that would settle over them in those moments, when they stood shoulder to shoulder—whether they called each other balije, ustaše, or četnici with bitter irony and resentment—yet silently shared the same darkness. Terms such as **balije, ustaše,** and *četnici* were often used during the war and its aftermath to label opposing sides, but they carry deeply derogatory and divisive meanings and are recognized today as offensive slurs.

Everyone carried their own thoughts, their fears, and their hopes, and yet they shared what they had, as if aware that solidarity was their only salvation.

For Dall, war became daily life, an inseparable part of her childhood and family story. She grew used to the sounds of ambulance sirens, warnings of incoming attacks, the thunder of shells shattering nearby, the damp and moldy cellars where they hid, and the shards of shrapnel that buried themselves into walls. To her, this was normal—just as mobile phones and the internet are to children today.

While political leaders schemed to seize as much as they could, robbing their people, they neither grasped nor could extinguish the primal resilience of the Bosnian spirit. That spirit, which had endured through centuries—woven of survival, love, and grief—lived on in the stories and verses of giants like Meša Selimović, whose The Fortress, and Death and the Dervish spoke of struggle and inner conflict, or Ivo Andrić, our Nobel laureate, whose Letter from 1920 still echoes through time. Dall loved those writers; she found in them the resonance of her own soul. All that blood, all that love and hatred, two irreconcilable forces intertwining on the Balkans—that was a great enigma no outsider could ever truly understand. In that mixture of sorrow, pain, and hope, Dall found the strength to believe in a better tomorrow, to believe in life and in people.

Because even as grenades thundered and the world around her collapsed, people still showed their most beautiful human qualities—solidarity, love, and compassion. And it was precisely in that extraordinary togetherness, in that silence of shared pain and hope, that Dall saw and preserved her small world of light.

On the other hand, the peoples of the Balkans often wasted their lives searching for that "golden middle," without realizing how, from early childhood, a poisonous hatred was being instilled into many.

Paradoxically, those who remained trapped in such a predetermined system found it easiest. Those who were a little more literate, who understood the complexity of the world around them, were deeply worried about their children's future. They wandered, searching for a way out, desiring a better fate, but often lost themselves in endless paths of uncertainty.

All this unfolded in a land that was once a symbol of resistance to fascism, a land of magical pastures and dense forests, a land where sevdah once echoed— filled with sorrow and beauty. And yet, why does it seem that the heritage we carry is burdened with blood, pain, and bitterness? How could a place that was once a cradle of civilization and literacy now bear such tragedy?

The tragicomic fact is that while some pretended to be civilized citizens, feigning to understand the world, it was the illiterate and semi-literate who directly and indirectly led to the downfall of this country and its society. Illiteracy played a key role in the disintegration of the former state, because an uneducated people are easy prey for manipulation by the media and false leaders.

It is well known that life in the Balkans, over the last hundred years and three bloody wars, has been filled with tragedy. History has mercilessly played with all of us, leaving behind deep wounds and divisions that even today are difficult to heal.

And so, the question remains: what is it that we, as the generation that lives and breathes here today, will leave to our children? Will we leave them a legacy of fear, hatred, and uncertainty? Or will we, somehow, even in the smallest steps, find the strength to give them hope, love, and the chance to build a world different from the one we inherited?

Each of us, in our own way, chooses what we will pass on to future generations.

In that Balkan war, it was never about the number of people killed—that figure is utterly irrelevant. In the Bosnian War, the scale of killings was tragic, but equally important were the motives, objectives, methods, and the systematic targeting of civilians across Bosnia and Herzegovina.

During the war, some of the bloodiest crimes in modern history took place in Bosnia. And while war is most often told as a man's story, here it came to women in the worst and most brutal of forms.

Unlike earlier wars, fought differently, this Balkan postmodern war was unique because it entered urban areas—into homes and streets themselves. Rape, as a horrific tool of war, was not only meant to humiliate victims, but also to demonstrate power and mark territory. Dall would forever be grateful that she never had to witness such a painful, dehumanizing act.

By seventh grade, though physically the tiniest—thin, undernourished, a frail little girl—Dall was intellectually more mature than her peers. The way she had grown up, in a reality opposite to the fairy tales she loved to read, had taught her to pull something good even from the hardest situations.

She never came home to repeat the insults or cruel names her classmates called her—as a child of mixed parentage. She bore it all stoically, ignoring the mockery until those who ganged up on her eventually gave up.

Today, happiness seems like a complicated concept, dependent on countless factors. But back then, Dall learned to value the smallest things.

Her first great happiness was the night electricity returned. The first snowflakes wet her cheeks as she spun in the street with a few neighbors, twirling and laughing in delight. The streetlights glowed, ending years spent in darkness.

Chapter 6

Life after War

Bugojno, Bosnia and Herzegovina, 1995

The Dayton Agreement was signed at the end of 1995. Mira and Dall were living as tenants in a neighborhood near the elementary school "Vojin Paleksić," which Dall attended.

A small, damp room in a stone house was enough for Mira and Dall, but it was not a permanent solution.

Still, as Mira always said: in life, good and bad things happen to us, but we choose whether we experience them as good or bad.

In the end, the choice is always ours.

It is not a shame to hit rock bottom. The shame is in not rising from it, in blaming others, in wasting your energy in the wrong direction.

For Dall, eighth grade passed relatively well—she grew closer to a few classmates, mostly boys. Puberty had already touched most of the girls in her class, but not Dall. She preferred comfort and simplicity— tracksuits, T-shirts, and soccer were closer to her heart than any feminine clothing.

She even wore glasses, often disregarding the conventions of how a girl should look.

It is hard to live in small, tense communities where everyone knows everything about everyone. Places where the main pastime of the idle is meddling in other people's lives. Where, if you are not polite and "proper" by their standards, you are somehow sanctioned, and life is made harder for you.

As someone different from the accepted norm, every step of Dall's was followed, her mistakes and flaws sought out. Even those closest to her sometimes betrayed or gossiped, searching for anything to use against her.

Dall enviously and defiantly guarded her privacy. She never spoke of life's hardships, nor did she allow anyone to pry into where or how she and Mira lived. That secrecy and distance were an even bigger thorn in the side of her nosy peers.

She fell into the category of girls with delayed puberty. While today puberty often begins earlier, back then it was quite normal for a thirteen-year-old girl to only begin showing the first signs.

Small and frail, she felt surrounded by giants.

Other girls were already wearing bras, styling their hair, and inventing fashion trends. All of that was unimportant to her—until her first crush was born.

He bore her father's name and lived in the same neighborhood—Donjići—as Dall. Alongside him and his brother, there were Julia and her brother Tare, and their mutual friend Kan.

The days suddenly became too short for everything Dall, Julia, Kan, and Sajo wanted to do together. They spent all their free time as one, and whatever they could not finish in daylight, they extended deep into the night...

What especially connected Dall and her crush was playing tennis. For hours they practiced their swings, perfected their serves, shouted and argued with each other, and then, exhausted, went home. Sajo was a handsome and confident boy, unafraid to come to Dall's door and shout for her to come outside if she had the time.

When first crushes appear, children often do not know how to express them, especially in front of their parents, but Mira's watchful eye missed nothing. She often teased Dall yet still allowed her to talk to her as a mother, giving her advice on this or that. Like every young girl, Dall naively and idealistically believed in mutual understanding and respect, even when it came to matters of affection.

Once, during a game of hide-and-seek, Sajo suggested a rule: when someone found him, he would have to write the name of his crush on a piece of paper and give it to the finder. On that paper appeared two names. Dall felt disappointed, even though one of them was hers. That moment shook her confidence. She began to look for faults in herself—thinking about how she was not as developed as other girls, how she had nothing nice to wear, and so on.

In the end, Dall decided to step aside and "give" her crush to Julija—the second name on the note. She thought: "If he already wants someone else besides me, let him have her." She began inventing excuses each time Sajo invited her to play tennis. Eventually, it turned out that Julija liked Kan, and Sajo, in wanting too much, lost the friendship of both girls.

Mira and Dall lived in Donjići until the end of the school year, when they relocated to the house of Momčilo, the man who owned the property, near the Vesela neighborhood. Dall longed to enroll in the famous Bugojno Gymnasium and spent that summer vacation preparing day and night for the entrance exam.

That same summer, puberty finally arrived. The skinny, frail girl transformed into an elegant swan, almost a head taller than her peers, who teased and bragged about themselves in eighth grade. Mira did everything she could, surviving as best she knew how.

Life was still harsh, but for Dall, high school marked the beginning of an entirely new chapter.

The Gymnasium in Bugojno, built during the Austro- Hungarian Monarchy, was a true architectural gem with its pseudo-Moorish style. In the 1960s, it bore the name of Mahmut Bušatlija, a national hero from Bugojno, and after the war it was renamed the Bugojno Gymnasium. Most of the children walked to and from school every day. At that time, there were no mobile phones, so every step of the way home was an opportunity to discover small details, little wonders, and encounters with a world slowly waking up from long years of darkness.

Although the war years were behind them, forgotten grenades and bombs still lay scattered in backyards and passageways—dangers everyone knew they must not touch. Parents warned their children not to pick up anything they found on the ground and not to wander into tall grass. They told frightening stories about those who had disobeyed boys who had paid a terrible price for their carelessness.

It was a period when life was slowly regaining color. The city resounded with the first chords of rock 'n' roll music, a sign that the darkness was finally retreating. Yet tensions and uncertainty did not disappear overnight. War scars ran deep, and many had lost their homes. In mixed marriages, suspicions and divisions still smoldered.

Bugojno was a town of many emigrants who despite the distance, maintained bridges with their families through financial help and care packages, giving them strength and hope during hard days. Unemployment was high, and neighborhoods devastated by war looked like ruins, with demolished buildings and scarred façades bearing witness to past injustice and suffering. Bribery had, unfortunately, become an everyday reality—small envelopes hidden in pockets or bags solved many obstacles, from traffic fines to waiting in doctors' offices.

Such was life in post-war Bugojno, where people still tried to find their balance in a world that had changed, yet somehow stayed the same. People nonetheless socialized much more, unburdened by social media and mobile phones. Although civilization had advanced greatly compared to the distant year of 1996, people had become dulled by modern technology apathetic. Without those distractions, people back then were not addicts to screens and, in every sense, lived better—they spent more time outside, were more active, and more joyful.

That same year, like many other refugees, Ibro returned home—to his native town on the Vrbas River. The ordeals he had survived had changed him; they had somehow broken the great and strong man Dall once remembered. His family home had been burned and destroyed, and within it had perished many of Mira's and Dall's childhood memories. Upon his return, Ibro settled with his wife Safa and their youngest son in his brother's house, and Dall and Mira often visited these returnees.

One way or another, the Bugojno Gymnasium was attended by children of, let us say, slightly wealthier parents. There were children of ministers, professors, doctors, politicians—but of course also a handful of "strays" like Dall or Sema, a few refugees here and there, though such students were rare in those times.

As a little girl, Dall had been hyperactive. She had trouble sitting still to study, her mind in constant chaos, always thinking of something else. She would study aloud, pacing kilometers around her room— something that helped her focus on the material. High school wasn't much easier, but with age she had learned to cope better.

Since she did not come from a wealthy family, she had no material possessions of value, which made it hard to fit in. She got along more easily with boys, since the girls had already formed cliques from the very beginning—based on this or that—in which Dall never belonged. She hated questions about her private life, rarely opened, and that sense of not fitting in followed her throughout life.

As a child, she often asked herself why some people seemed to have the ability to adapt so easily in different situations, while she did not. Was it a matter of weak social intelligence, or of how others perceived her? In short, Dall feared rejection—more than she longed to belong to something she wasn't. To live in that "fitted-in" skin was suffocating—that false skin broke her wings—and that was exactly how Dall felt at the start of high school.

Her homeroom teacher was a chemistry professor: balding, red-cheeked, middle-aged—strict.

Interestingly, the biology teacher was the wife of her former physics teacher, Drago the Montenegrin, whom Dall had admired back in elementary school. The biology teacher was infamous as the strictest professor—one whom no one could ever satisfy. And yet, perhaps because of memories, and because of the way Drago (her former teacher) had recognized and nurtured her potential, Dall sincerely respected and even loved her. She also loved the subject itself, and worked hard not to disappoint her, striving to show her knowledge.

The professor of language and literature was none other than their longtime acquaintance—Anton. Dall was not sure whether to be glad about this discovery or nervous. In typical teenage fashion, she worried that Anton would seize every opportunity to "rat her out" to Mira, or that she would never manage to meet his high expectations—at least where she was concerned.

As mentioned earlier, the name recorded on her birth certificate was Emre, and under that name she was enrolled in all school documents. Still, from about the fifth grade onward, teachers and children began using the name Dall, which she preferred. Only those closest to her—those who had known her since childhood— called her Dall, lovingly, like a nickname. Anton was one of them. He too must have been puzzled by the confusion around her name, but he never spoke of it. He addressed her in the way he was accustomed when they talked privately, while in formal situations he used the name listed in the school register.

Mira never wanted Dall to stand out from the others in any way, so she always made sure to provide her with clothing and shoes that were in fashion at the time. In appearance, Dall already looked like a young woman. Always talkative and lively, cheerful in spirit, Dall enjoyed the sympathy of most teachers. A brown- haired girl with dark, sparkling eyes and a fair complexion, sprinkled with tiny freckles and a sincere, warm smile—she was gladly accepted among her peers.

Of medium height, with a nicely shaped figure, she attracted the attention of boys, even if she couldn't be described as a classic beauty. She was not a straight-A student, but she usually finished the year with B grades. As usual, the natural sciences did not interest her much, and she fought hard to scrape by with Cs in chemistry, physics, and mathematics. Languages such as Bosnian, English, German, and Latin, as well as philosophy, were her strengths, while biology and geography were always solid B's.

Somewhere in the second year of gymnasium, Dall grew close to Doli. A quiet, withdrawn girl who came from an old Bugojno family. She had an older sister, Stela, living in Italy, and she too belonged to the category of "the others." As a child of a mixed marriage, she and Dall quickly found common ground. Doli—an artistic soul, who would spend hours sketching abstract drawings that Dall admired, even though she had no real understanding of art—was the opposite of Dall. While Dall was cheerful, constantly in motion, and naturally talkative, Doli was introverted, quiet, a calm harbor. Yet somehow, they complemented each other—sharing their deepest secrets, giving advice, and helping each other walk more easily through high school.

Halfway through that school year, in the second grade, Mira and Dall faced a new move—a new life challenge. Momčilo, their landlord, notified them that the property had been sold and that they were required to vacate the premises without delay. The idea of changing schools never even crossed Dall's mind. She felt a wave of nausea at every mention of possibly going to a completely new environment, which quickly turned into anger at the very thought that she and Mira had to start over again.

Chapter 7

When Love First Spoke

Bugojno, Bosnia and Herzegovina, 1997 Donji Vakuf, Bosnia and Herzegovina, 1998-2002

Outside of school, Dall was almost always with Sanči, who grew up between an older brother and an older sister. The sister was married to a policeman and lived in Donji Vakuf, while the brother still lived at home. Sanči was an average student at a vocational trade school, but hanging out with her was more than entertaining. While Sanči was not too concerned about school, Dall had her days when she had to study certain subjects no matter what. Still, there was some balanced harmony between them.

Dall and Sanči together attended the first post-war concert of Mladen Vojičić—Tifa—in Bugojno in 1997, after days and nights of negotiations and pleas to Mira to let her go. Sanči had already gotten permission and money from her parents. It was their first independent evening outing—something both would remember for the rest of their lives.

Never again did Dall feel such adrenaline—such a crowd of people, such an atmosphere and euphoria. People were jumping, screaming, singing—it was complete chaos. As if everyone was trying to release in a single breath year of accumulated frustrations, war losses, joy, and sorrow all at once.

Next to Dall knelt a young man with a red band tied around his forehead. Sanči was convinced it was someone they knew—or at least someone who resembled him. No matter how hard they tried, they could not figure out whether the young man was crying or singing. All around them alcohol had been spilled, shards of glass scattered across the floor. Sanči quietly gestured to Dall to tell him to get up before he cut himself. Dall mustered up her courage and tapped him on the shoulder—only then did the stranger raise his head.

He was not anyone they had ever seen before, but his eyes—piercing, dreamy—left a deep mark in Dall's memory. They often reappeared in her dreams, long after Tifa's concert.

Still, despite all efforts and "detective" attempts the two girls they never managed to find out who that mysterious young man really was. At the time, it was almost shameful for girls their age to enter cafés, so Dall and Sanči did not dare investigate the Bugojno hangouts on their own. That is why Sanči came up with a new idea—to go to Donji Vakuf, "for a coke with whipped cream." Supposedly, there was a very popular café there called **Café Cloud**, where a waiter worked who had completely stolen Sanči's heart.

According to plan, one afternoon after school they met at the bus station. They boarded an old Servistrans bus and headed toward the little town on the Vrbas River. The distance between the two towns was about 12 kilometers, so the ride did not take long. Bravely, they stepped into the café, sat down, and ordered small Cokes topped with whipped cream from the famous waiter, chatting happily.

Sanči, of course, had the usual questions—was he looking at her or not—while Dall, a little bored, gazed around the place. Nele, the waiter, was quick, skillful with words, cheerful by nature—one of those so-called "players." He joked, stuffed his mouth with whipped cream, teased Sanči to try some—the atmosphere was easy and relaxed.

In that whole game of cat and mouse, Dall felt uncomfortable, as if she were technically an extra, and she could not wait to get outside. Just then, a white Golf with the sticker "**Café Cloud**" pulled up in front of the café. Someone was unloading crates of soda and beer, stacking them neatly into the storeroom. The young man who walked in clearly had authority—Nele instantly "put on" the mask of a professional, serious waiter in his presence.

The stranger was dressed casually. Tall, broad- shouldered, he stood out in the crowd, and his dark, almost black hair was neatly trimmed in a military style. At first glance, he seemed a bit surly, maybe even arrogant, but at the same time strangely mysterious. He was certainly over twenty. Dark- skinned, with thin lips, a serious face, and chestnut- brown eyes... the very same chestnut eyes that had haunted Dall in her dreams ever since that unforgettable Tifa's concert.

Dall froze, silently watching his body language, the thud of his steps, the swift, precise way his hands moved as he sorted the deliveries. He radiated a quiet yet powerful energy. He was not a classically handsome man, but he carried with him masculinity, charisma, and that elusive something that wordlessly takes over a room and commands attention. He had the posture of a man who knew exactly who he was, where he was going, and to whom he owed no explanations. Confidence and charm exuded from his every move, even as he stacked crates in the storeroom.

His gaze drifted casually across the nearly empty room, lingering now and then on Dall, who, caught off guard, frantically tried to calm her racing thoughts and heart.

"Who's that?" she whispered as soon as Nele returned to their table.

"The boss," he replied with a half-smile. "In charge of everything—supplies, staff, the business. He runs this place. The actual owner is more of a figurehead, here just to collect the money and leave."

"I was just asking..." Dall stammered, trying to sound indifferent. "He looked familiar."

Nele grinned knowingly. "Watch out for him. He is dangerous—especially with the ladies. Guys like him do not come with warning signs... they break hearts easily."

Dall theatrically rolled her eyes, trying to cover the storm raging inside her. She smiled, but inside she was in turmoil. Names had always meant a lot to her. She believed they were more than labels—they carried stories, destinies, perhaps even fragments of character. If you wanted to truly know someone, she often said, find out the meaning of their name. The real meaning. The origin. The etymology. And she always marveled at how much truth could be hidden in a single name.

And his name... it matched everything he embodied— his stance, his appearance, that unspoken authority.

The name of a warrior. The name of someone who did not ask permission to be noticed.

"Nele, wrap this up," that deep voice rang out, clear and commanding. "I have to go."

Dall did not even blink. She just stared. Sanči glanced at her with her playful blue eyes and mischievously winked, as if she knew everything—even what Dall had not yet admitted to herself. Dall loved that mischievous side of Sanči, and even when she tried hard to stay serious, she often could not hold back laughter that suddenly released the lump in her throat.

From that afternoon on, trips to **Café Cloud** became more frequent, and Dall used every opportunity to spend weekends at Ibro and Safa's house. Little by

little, a few of the people who had fled the Vrbas area during the war began to return home. That is how Dall soon reunited with a couple of childhood friends— Lejla and Sarah.

Sarah had returned with her parents from Germany and lived two houses away from Ibro's family. A chubby, sharp-tongued, blue-eyed teenager, she quickly won the hearts of everyone around her. Lejla was the eldest child of Jim and Rana. Jim had married her mother when Lejla was only three years old, and soon they had three more children. They lived on the edge of survival, but somehow managed to get by.

Lejla's two half-brothers were developmentally delayed, and her little half-sister was still just a child, so there was not much closeness among them. Lejla was essentially her mother's child—she always had something to wear and to eat, while the others came after, if there was anything left for them. It was a very different life from the old Donja Mahala where Dall had grown up, but over time people slowly began to return to their homes.

As she wrestled with the whirlwind of emotions that consumed her, Dall confided mostly in Doli. Mira tirelessly searched for an apartment until, somehow, the solution practically presented itself. That weekend Mira and Dall were visiting Ibro and his family. Dall had been sent to the store, and on her way, a large white transporter stopped. One of the soldiers shouted: "Does anyone speak English?"

Dall hesitantly approached the vehicle and started a conversation. It turned out the soldiers were Dutch and that one of their military bases would be established at the very entrance to Donji Vakuf. At first, they were looking for a woman to work in the kitchen, and later they would also need a cleaner. Without hesitation, Dall suggested her mother, explaining that Mira had worked in hospitality and kitchens for many years and was surely the best candidate. Lieutenant Gail joked that Dall should introduce him to her mother, adding that at least they would not have translation problems, and their problem was solved.

Mira was not thrilled with the idea—she complained she would not be able to communicate successfully, that they were all young men, and so on. But with Dall's insistence, she finally gave in. The offered salary was more than enough for a decent life, and soon the employment contract was signed.

Ibro and Safa tirelessly urged Mira to move to Donji Vakuf. "You're looking for an apartment anyway," Ibro would say. "The son of our late friend is renting out a small ground-floor flat. It is perfect for you and Dall to start." Dall, who already spent most of her free time with them, silently celebrated the plan. They also spoke with Erdo, the deposit for rent was paid, and the move could begin.

Dall wanted to continue her schooling in Bugojno, and public transportation was her only option. Although she hated buses and crowds, she was ready to make that small sacrifice. She firmly believed that women chose men who were either replicas of their fathers or their complete opposites. The stranger with chestnut eyes often drove around in his white Golf, window rolled down, frequently exchanging glances with Dall.

Café Cloud had no competition. On weekends, crowds were so big that guests waited even on the stairs to get inside. There were only one or two other cafés at the time, but everything seemed to revolve around **Café Cloud**. The stranger was often surrounded by young women, all seeking his attention and affection. Dall was not sure she liked that, so she decided to firmly bury any feelings of infatuation and follow a different path. Her goal was clear—finish school and find a way to pursue university.

During summer vacation, she worked to earn pocket money. Jan, a young man three years older, approached her one evening wanting to meet. He explained that ever since Dall had lived in Bugojno, he had been waiting outside the mixed school for months, just to catch sight of her as she walked home.

Dall hated that route, mostly because the Police Academy was near the Tajči tavern. Boys came there from all over Bosnia, and some were rude with whistles and catcalls, so Dall always hurried to pass that stretch on her way to the roundabout.

Soon their outings grew into a friendship, and then into Dall's first relationship. Jan came from a patriarchal family and was one of those people who had his entire life planned out—from high school to university, employment, marriage, and even the choice of his future wife. At the time, customs did not allow young couples to openly show affection. They would walk side by side, hands in their pockets, slowly getting to know one another and enjoying each other's presence.

Throughout high school, Dall spent most of her free time with Jan. They attended concerts, enjoyed excursions, and took long evening walks. He was a quiet refuge for Dall, her complete opposite. Dall wanted to live life to the fullest, to travel, see the world, and experience different cultures.

She could not imagine herself as someone who would spend her entire life in a small town, enslaved to a husband, aunts, a mother-in-law, and everyone else. She firmly believed that men and women were equal, that education had a purpose—to build a family together, supporting and complementing one another.

But the Balkan mentality at that time was very different. The woman was responsible for the house and children, while the man was the main provider. Men went out and participated in social events, while women were expected to be content with whatever small amount of attention they were given.

Working in a café taught Dall enough lessons for two lifetimes—but it also made clear what she wanted, and what she never wanted, for her future.

High school flew by in a blink. Jan enrolled in Forestry in Sarajevo, while Dall, lacking the means for university, stayed behind to work a year or two to save up the necessary funds. Hot summer evenings brought the amusement park as a small oasis of entertainment in the town on the Vrbas. Nele, who had in time become a good friend of Dall's, took her and Lejla to the carousel, as a little escape from the bustle of the city. Dall never liked spinning in circles, but she agreed. As the rides went on, she felt worse.

When the carousel finally stopped, she was so sick she had to lie down to the side, unable to move.

From the shadows, a pair of chestnut eyes stared at her, with a remark that children should not be riding, or something along those lines.

It turned out he worked in security. Dall pretended to be deaf and mute, ignoring his comments, but as soon as she realized her legs would not carry her anymore, she quietly asked to leave. Back at **Café Cloud**, the chestnut eyes had completely taken over Dall's attention and emotions, leaving her breathless and under their quiet influence. That evening they sat for hours, chatting about everything and nothing, and despite her efforts to stay composed, Dall longingly lost herself in those deep eyes. Age no longer mattered, the whole world disappeared—for even though she knew there was no turning back, Dall had neither the strength nor the will to resist those piercing chestnut glances.

No love ever happens by accident, whether attraction strikes at first sight or waits for years—that does not matter. In both cases, something happens in the Universe to bring two people together, to love, to bond. No one has ever—and probably never will— find a magical formula, a single word that perfectly describes love as a result.

Love is strange, it clouds reason, tangles all other feelings, as if it drains every bit of sense you possess. It offers the deepest bliss, and in return it asks only for your heart. At the same time, it can strike the hardest, create agony and suffering in the most hidden corners of the soul. No matter how many poems, sonnets, and epics have been written, no great writer has yet managed to capture that silent storm of feelings that has tormented humanity since the dawn of time.

For Dall, this love was turbulent, full of ups and downs, arguments, longing, passion, unfulfilled desires, joy, and pain. To her, it was pure, naïve, almost childlike—unconditional. There was no list of expectations or perfections her partner had to meet. She loved the whole imperfect being, just as he was, with all his virtues and flaws.

He had grown up mostly with his grandparents. One day his mother realized that life with his father in a small provincial town was not what she truly wanted, so she moved abroad with someone who suited her heart better. His father later remarried and had two daughters. He matured on the rough streets, in an environment of war's horrors and dangers. He built an impenetrable fortress around his heart, afraid of being abandoned, hurt. He did not know how to give himself completely, nor to surrender fully to one woman.

The person we fall for, the one we feel powerful emotions toward, often becomes our ideal. And so, all of Dall's thoughts were intertwined with him, colored by emotions. Everything that belonged to him, Dall saw in a better light—as something superior, unattainable, like an intriguing riddle she had to solve. She believed in his brighter side, allowing herself to dream, to justify, to deceive her own heart, hoping that the force of her love would overcome all obstacles despite every sign pointing otherwise.

Emotionally unavailable partners are often like closed books—charming, entertaining, beloved in society, but still guarding hidden corners of their soul from others. That was her stranger too: interesting, witty, attractive, but distant, as if some invisible barrier separated him from real intimacy. His closed-off nature was not just a quirk or a choice—it was almost constant, rarely sharing emotions, rarely speaking of the past.

When you spend time with such a person, even though moments are filled with laughter and ease, there always remains an indelible sense that something is missing, something you cannot quite grasp—as if there is always an invisible wall in their presence.

That difficulty in expressing love was not merely his weakness but the consequence of deep childhood wounds, of emptiness he did not know how to fill.

No story was ever clear, because Dall never really learned the truth. Had he grown up around figures of authority who did not know how to provide safety and warmth when he needed it most? Was it instilled in him from an early age that he must be strong, brave, never show weakness, that crying was a sign of weakness, and sadness something to be hidden?

Whatever the case, Dall's teenage years were not enough for her to grasp the depth of his pain nor to understand whether such a relationship could ever hold real, healthy closeness. She learned that with someone like him, perhaps it was unwise to expect too much connection—because from such closeness a deep wound can too easily emerge, one that hurts and does not heal for a long time.

It is hard to face the truth and admit to yourself that the person you idealized so much may not be ready for the kind of relationship you want. Harder still is facing the fact that we always have a choice—that it is our decision that shapes our lives. It is easier to blame the entire male gender, to shift responsibility to others, than to clear your mind and admit to yourself that you are the one steering your path.

But real strength lies in being ready to take responsibility for your life, to accept your choices, and move forward, stronger, and wiser. No man, no woman, can be possessed. Love is not a chain, not an obligation to fulfill a checklist of desires or conditions.

Love is freedom—to love someone without expectations, without reproaches, without those quiet tallies that silently carve distance between hearts. In true love there is not much wisdom, not too much reason, no textbook to learn from. No one has ever taught us how to love, yet we think we know—we love what gives us comfort, call it love, while true love comes quietly, without questions and without rules.

When that primal feeling truly seizes you, you realize love has no boundaries. It simply is. You love without asking why, without counting how much you will get in return. Our conscious and subconscious choose people and situations we need in that exact moment—and although it may seem incomprehensible, almost contrary to cosmic law, Dall chose him. Without expectations, without judgment.

It is hard to accept that tango always takes two—our instinct is to believe we are right, that it is all on us, that our love is enough.

Only when we are brave enough to face the truth can we forgive and move on.

And the stranger who stole Dall's heart? He belonged to her, to me, to you, to everyone—and yet, at the same time, only to himself, and to no one.

Dall often felt deep frustration, reflecting on how many of us are loved conditionally—by parents, family, society. We were not taught to understand and nurture our emotions, but instead prepared with defense mechanisms that appear when we do not know how else to express or protect ourselves. Parents, often unconsciously, passed on the message that love meant to endure, to tolerate, to carry the weight of others' emotions, even when it was not our fault. Children followed rules and demands not because they wanted to, but because they had to—because they were told so.

Because of these dysfunctional patterns, we search in partners for what we lacked in childhood—we try to heal the emptiness, to satisfy the hunger of an unmet emotional need. Perhaps that was why Dall was drawn to an emotionally unavailable man, just as she herself carried burdens she did not fully understand.

Dall did not like to share private things; she avoided unnecessary questions and open conflicts. She was reserved, confiding in only a rare few. Yet she believed that every mistake brings us closer to who we really are and what we truly deserve. She believed that what bothers one person in us could become the very reason another person loves us. Everyone who crosses our path carries a lesson we need to learn, and right where we are—in that place, in that moment—is exactly where we are meant to be.

Their paths diverged. And if they ever did cross for a moment, it was the most beautiful illusion of nature, a mistake of the universe. They settled for brief encounters, knowing they were headed in opposite directions. They stole secret kisses, rushed into each other's arms only to part again, meeting once more at the crossroads of fate. Half of what Dall longed for from those chestnut eyes never came true. Maybe, someday, in another life, in a parallel universe, they would meet again as strangers who knew each other too well.

Until then, the old clock tower would remain the faithful witness to a lost love and a broken girl's heart. Most of Dall's life before college was spent with Almasa. Their unbreakable friendship was filled with a closeness rarely found—so strong that they became like family to one-anothe r.At a once-popular pizzeria, they worked side by side, sharing exhaustion and laughter, the scent of baked dough and youth. Behind closed doors, in quiet moments, they entrusted each other with the most intimate secrets of their young hearts. There, threads were woven that bound together their tears, dreams, and the small adventures that stay forever.

Almasa's life had never been easy. She grew up with a single mother and two sisters, in a home where hardworking hands and warm hearts made up for what was missing. Their everyday life was a struggle—they helped their mother, cared for the youngest sister, and walked through life together.

Their father, broken by the war and deteriorating mental health, caused a great family tragedy that led to Almasa's grandmother being shot in front of her, an event that shattered their home and marked its final collapse. In the chaos of war, Almasa was separated from her mother and sisters, who found refuge in Switzerland. Yet, as in rare but precious stories, fate eventually allowed them to reunite. After the war, they returned to Donji Vakuf—to the native valleys that had been waiting for them.

Almasa was sincere, sharp-tongued, hardworking, romantic by nature—but above all, warm-hearted and tireless in her feelings. To Dall, she was a sister of the soul. Together they grew up, sharing secrets forever etched into their hearts.

When Dall set off on her university path, their lives slowly began to drift apart, like rivers searching for their own course. Even then, they never broke the ties that bound them. Their friendship continued through stories, letters, and laughter with Almasa's sisters—all the way until Dall's life crossed the ocean to America.

What they shared never ceased to live on—it remained woven into her, like a quiet melody a person carries within, wherever they go.

Dall felt emotion like a sickle—held high, with respect and dignity—but also like a golden coin given stiffly, shyly, sparingly. Pieces of her soul were torn raw, left to heal on their own. The love of a young, naïve girl— almost still a child—remained forever etched in time, alongside those who hurt her and those she hurt, alongside the broken and the saviors.

Time did its work. She forgot what had wounded her, but not what it had taught her. Whatever the outcome, it had been worth it. People suffer from unacknowledged emotions because they are unable to face the traumas buried deep in their subconscious.

We are taught to suppress emotions, not to fully live them out. Love, sorrow, anger, pain—all demand to be lived, released, not suffocated. That is why we forgive so reluctantly, why we struggle to face reality, fighting the hardest battle of all—the battle with ourselves.

Dall vowed that her children would know how to express anger, to scream, to cry, to grieve when they were sad. She would teach them to care for their own feelings first, and only then for the feelings of others. She would never raise them to behave according to the expectations of the community, but according to themselves. For that is the true preservation of the inner child—that broken child who still lives within us today.

Why strive to be an honors student, a good athlete, an exemplary person, successful, a loyal friend—if you achieve all that but never once tend to your emotions when it matters most? Beneath all the layers the world has forced upon us, beneath the illusions of perfect families, lies life. But not the fairytale kind—the raw, brutal kind. Until you face yourself, there is no true healing.

Chapter 8

The City That Tested Her

Mostar, Bosnia and Herzegovina, 2002

It took Dall a long, far too long time to move past her prejudices, to put a period on long-shattered illusions, and to resist self-pity—one of the most destructive human emotions. That morning, for the first time, she stood up to her father decisively. She had never asked for anything, never begged for attention—not for a word, not for a glance. She had been a silent shadow on the edge of his thoughts, an invisible specter of his past that he carried like a scar beneath the skin. But now, for the first time in her life, she stood before him without blinking, without tears, without the silence that had rendered her invisible for years.

There was neither sorrow nor pleading in her eyes— only the stripped-bare contempt and resolve of a woman whom life had taught not to wait any longer.

"If you don't help me enroll at university, you will never see me again," she said coldly. Her voice did not shake. She did not beg. She left him not a sliver of space for excuses, or for new promises, or for fake tenderness. She shouted. She shouted everything she had kept silent for years. That she would sue him for every unpaid child support payment, for every year in which he called her "daughter" only when he needed to prove he had a heart. For every arrival with a false smile and every departure in silence. "Do not come here selling me castles in the air! I am not Mira, and I will not keep servicing your crap anymore!" she said straight to his face, without lowering her gaze. She was no longer the little girl who hoped her daddy would stay. The ultimatum was clear: bring the money for enrollment, then go. Do whatever you want, be a man somewhere else. Because here, you no longer exist.

And perhaps that was the first time it truly hurt him. Not because of the money. But because he had lost the only person who had silently waited for years for him to be a father. And when she finally spoke—it was too late.

She enrolled at the Pedagogical Faculty in Mostar— quietly, modestly, almost inaudibly, as if she herself could hardly believe she had succeeded—thanks mostly to her mother's support. The money for enrollment arrived grudgingly, with bitterness—as a drop that slipped from the hand of someone who never knew how to give with love. It was enough to enroll. Not enough for dignity.

While her roommates ordered coffee with laughter and planned their nights out, she counted coins and hid her shame in corners of her being where no one could see. She carried one bag, and she always said "thank you" too much—out of the habit of never taking anything for granted.

She was ashamed not of her poverty, but of having to ask. Of speaking her need aloud, with a knot in her stomach. And of the fact that the fulfillment of her dream depended on a plea. Her roommates understood it—or did not. They were good girls, but they did not know what it is when your voice breaks on "please," what it is when your cheeks burn as you quietly ask: "Do you maybe have any extra coffee?"

But Dall did not give up. In lectures she always sat in the front row. She read more than required, wrote with passion, studied through pain. Because she knew— the only way not to be ashamed one day is to go through all of it and remain proud, upright, at peace with yourself.

She did not seek pity. She only sought a chance. And she got it. Through her struggle, someone's indifference, and her faith in herself—which cost nothing and was worth everything.

Mostar is an ancient city—wondrous and quiet, yet powerful in its history and beauty.

A city of stone and water, of light and shadow, a place where time does not flow straight, but breaks and folds back, as if someone keeps reminding it of what once was.

At the heart of that city stands the Old Bridge—a stone arch that connects not only the banks of the Neretva, but centuries, people, stories, loves, wars, and forgiveness. A bridge that is not just a structure, but the soul of Mostar and a silence in which you can hear everything words cannot say.

It stands steadfast, drawing the gazes of tourists who touch the cold stone walls with reverence, as if they might whisper tales of dives from the bridge, of forgotten promises, of letters cast into the river and embraces at the crown of the arch—where the heart breaks most easily—and heals the fastest. They marveled at its primordial beauty, but did not realize that the beauty of the Old Bridge lies not only in its form, but in its stubbornness to rise, to endure, to bear witness. To survive.

Like her, Dall, who—just like the Old Bridge—learned how dignity rises from ruins, how strength is built in silence, and how hope is born from a gaze lifted to the sky—a hope that never again descends.

Meanwhile, tired of being everyone's mop and broom—because that is exactly how they treated her after she got a job with SFOR—Mira decided to turn her life around. **SFOR** was a NATO-led multinational peacekeeping force in Bosnia and Herzegovina.

It was established in December 1996, following the Dayton Peace Agreement, to oversee the implementation of the peace accord that ended the Bosnian War.

For years she had cleaned, quietly and without objection, watched foreign uniforms, commanders, bureaucrats, obeyed orders in a language she didn't fully understand, and swallowed her dreams while someone else's world smelled of security and a steady paycheck.

The tavern job that followed was harder still—she worked from morning until late into the night, even into the early hours, just to put Dall through school and pay the bills. One morning, as she was mopping the tavern floor, she looked out the window and decided—perhaps because of a tiredness that could no longer fit inside her, or because of everything she had lived through, who knows... She opened a small café. Not big, but warm. It bore a name made from her and Dall's initials—short, clear, concise. On a corner where people know each other by name, where coffee arrives with a smile, and where for the first time in many years she felt like somebody. Like a host, not a servant.

She believed, honestly and fervently, that her own business was safer, fairer, and that through that little wooden café she would receive more support than ever before—from life, from people, perhaps even from him. The one who was the quiet shadow of all her disappointments. But she did not ask for miracles, she asked only for a little respect. A little peace in the coffee she brewed with her own hands.

And one table—for all the unspoken sentences she carried inside. For Dall, Mostar was a new chapter—colorful, loud, exciting, and yet a harsh city that spares neither the young nor the brave. She left with a suitcase in one hand and dread in her heart—but also with the faith that something was beginning that would change the course of her life forever. And it did.

But not the way she had imagined. There were many trials—the big city offered both lights and shadows. Distractions were everywhere: nights out that smelled of forgetting, people full of promises but empty of soul, moments of weakness when it seemed it would be easier just to let everything go. But Dall could not. Not for herself—but for her.

For Mira.

For her mother—for the woman who carried too much, gave all she had, and never asked anything in return except that her daughter be all right.

That is why Dall pushed on. She clenched her teeth when there was nothing to eat, when she studied at night and worked by day to pay not only for books, but for everything a life without safety entails: rent, utilities, even a ticket home she could seldom afford.

She did not want to share those burdens. She did not want Mira ever to know that her daughter cried into her pillow countless nights because she did not know how to bear the injustices and because no one had told her, "It will get easier."

Because she knew that her mother would sell even her last keepsake just to ease her pain. Mira had carried the burden for too long and it was too heavy. And Dall knew it. So, she fought—quietly, resolutely, relentlessly. Because her struggle was not just for a diploma.

It was for the dignity of their story. For something, at last, to end differently—not in pain, but in victory.

She cleared the first year of university. Without fanfare, without celebration, without any pomp. Quietly—with relief in her chest, a tear in her eye, and an unspoken "on we go" that she whispered to herself in the mirror. She often ran —literally—between lectures and her job at the souvenir shop.

Sometimes she fell asleep on her study notes, waking to an alarm that sounded like a reminder that dreams do not come easily.

She knew the way from the faculty to work by heart, every crack in the hot Mostar asphalt, every hour in which she had to choose—sleep or study. There were days she arrived at lectures utterly exhausted and everything in her head screamed to give up.

That she did not have to. That maybe it was all too much. But she did not. Because in those moments, when she looked at her student index with her name written inside, with professors' signatures and stamps of passed exams, she saw something bigger than herself. She saw her mother, Mira's look when it said: "I'm proud."

She saw all the work, all the silence and pain that brought her there. She knew she did not have the luxury of giving up. Not because she "had to," but because she had promised.

It would have been selfish to abandon her dreams when they were the one thing no one could take from her. So, she kept going.

With all her wounds, her fatigue, and her silence, because she knew this was not the end. This was only the first page of a story she would one day, sure of herself, tell to those who also thought they could not.

It's important to note that Dall was studying physics/mathematics/computer science. A course of study that had nothing to do with her, with her being, with what her soul had whispered since childhood.

Because she dreamed of books—of sentences that change lives—of days spent writing, in stories, seeking truth through words. She wanted to study literature or journalism—to be the one who asks, reflects, connects the world through language. But they told her: "Do not be foolish. Do not be another starving artist. That is not a life. That is ruin."

And so, she took what was on offer. Not what she loved, but what was "smart." And she did it with a knot in her throat. With a lump each time she opened a textbook on linear algebra or tried to slip into the abstract world of algorithms that said nothing to her— except that she was losing herself in something that had never been hers. She sat exams, regularly, punctually, even with good grades. But not one brought that feeling of being in the right place. Not one sparked a flame.

Everything was somehow limp, colorless, mechanical. Behind every good mark stood an emptiness, the quiet realization that each day she was further from herself. That was her great mistake—not because she was not capable, but because she betrayed what she believed in. Because she agreed to a life she did not feel.

And all the while, Mira labored selflessly in her café, firmly believing her child was on a safe path. While everyone said, "Bravo, physics! Computer science! A secure future!" No one asked her, "Are you happy?"

Hungry to be entirely herself, to be given a chance, to have a life that was not only a struggle to survive.

The second year of university was even harder—harder on every possible level: physically, mentally, emotionally. The coursework grew harsher and more abstract. Formulas and problems were no longer just school hurdles, but constant reminders that she was not where she wanted to be. As if every subject whispered, "You don't belong here."

The job she had could no longer cover even the basics, so she had to change jobs. The new one was more demanding—longer shifts, heavier physical work, less sleep. Her body slipped into autopilot while her mind spun with the same question, like a mantra: "Did I make a mistake choosing this path?"

The worst of all was Descriptive Geometry. She was not a bad student; she was not lazy. But every time she opened the book, she felt powerless. Lines, planes, and projections blended in her head, and nothing she tried seemed to work. Tutors existed, but not for her world. She could not afford extra lessons. Her money went first to rent, then to food, and if anything remained—maybe to life.

At the university, she learned quietly from classmates, soaking up knowledge from their words, taking notes, listening without asking questions so she would not look weak. Sometimes someone would sit beside her and help—not because of her, but out of that occasional, random kindness among students.

Every evening, returning to her room exhausted, she would look at her notes and ask herself: "How much longer can I go on like this? How long can I fight for something that does not fulfill me and costs more than I must give?"

But quitting was not an option. She did not have the luxury to stop. Behind her stood Mira, her mother, and an entire life that would not allow dreams to go out. So, she kept going. She did not shine, but she did not falter either. She was still there—and under these circumstances, that was a victory.

The feeling of not belonging—chasing her for years— did not disappear when she reached university; it grew louder. Everyone around her seemed to know exactly where they were headed. Children of ministers, lawyers, professors—people with security and families pushing them forward, with last names that opened doors even before they spoke.

And Dall? She had only her mother and a name that meant nothing to anyone but herself. She did not belong to their world. She did not understand their conversations about trips home, about family gatherings with uncles, aunts, grandmothers, and grandfathers. So, she withdrew. She didn't seek friendships that smelled of flattery. She kept to herself—quietly and with dignity. She knew she wasn't worth less—she had just been thrown into the fire differently.

But her life outside the faculty was a completely different world. Among the roommates she met in Mostar, Dall finally began to breathe. These were not girls with silicone plans and daddy's connections. They knew what it meant to count coins at the end of the month, shared makeup and recipes for meals made of "nothing," and laughed from the belly even when they knew they would cry under the covers that night.

With them, she went out for cheap coffees, student parties, and long walks under the Old Bridge. In those moments, she felt alive. Not rich, not special, but enough herself to forget everything that set her apart from others. There, she did not have to perform. She did not have to explain her past or why she didn't have much. They were together, and that was enough.

It was then she learned something no university could teach belonging is not about social class or last names. Belonging is a look that says, "I understand you too."

On scorching Mostar asphalt, where summer singes both pavement and hearts, she forged friendships that would carry her through life. Not connections of convenience, nor the shallow smiles of lecture halls. Real friendships, born in moments when you have nothing but yourself—and someone recognizes that "nothing" as everything.

There were girls from Gacko who carried their heavy pasts like war backpacks but laughed as if spring burned inside them. With them she shared bread, tears, and nights when the power went out—when they could talk for hours without light, but with light in their eyes.

Then came the Mostar girls—bold, bright, open— wearing that southern charm that smells of stone and the south. They taught her to laugh louder, to swear sometimes, and that she did not always have to be strong. They drew her into city life, showed her the hidden alleys that are not on any map, and taught her to love Mostar—not through postcards, but through the people who animate it.

There were handsome Mostar boys too—dark-eyed, easygoing—the kind who bring you ćevapi at two in the morning and listen to your stories like you are the most important person in the world. Some remained only as memories, some in messages arriving years later— "Hey, remember those days?"—but a few stayed in her life forever, like brothers not born in the same house but in the same struggle to find yourself in a world that keeps pushing you away.

In that Mostar sun, among buildings that remember better days and people who do not pretend, she found what she had not found in any classroom: belonging. Not to a system, not to titles, not to a future drawn by others, but to hearts that accepted her exactly as she was—tired, uncertain, persistent, and alive.

By the end of the second year, Dall was on the edge. At the faculty they studied descriptive geometry and spatial projections—still a wall she could not climb— standing in her way like a mute proof that maybe she was not "meant for this." But giving up was not an option. She poured in everything she had. She slept four hours, ate on the go, and spent days studying the intersections of prisms through pyramids as if her life depended on it. And in a way, it did—on that exam depended her next steps, her sense of worth, all the effort she had invested, that quiet fight to prove to herself, and maybe to others, that she could, that she mattered, that she was not just "another village girl who won't get far."

She memorized drawings, practiced lines until her fingers went numb, and in every pause, she sketched a new life in her mind—even if only in imagination. But Professor Naum... it was as if he did not see her drawings or her effort. He looked at her. And he failed her—repeatedly. With little explanation. With no support. As if each failure was another way of saying, "This isn't for you."

Each time he said, "You didn't pass, miss," she did not cry in front of him. No—never. But as soon as she stepped out of the room, tears would burn her cheeks like the blazing Mostar asphalt in July. There was something deeply unjust in that rejection—not only because of the exam itself, but because the effort was never recognized. Because the system loves the strong—so long as they fit the mold. And she did not. She never did.

At the end of the second year, for who knows which time, she left Naum's office with emptiness in her chest, and then—maybe for the first time, honestly and out loud—she asked herself: "Am I here just to survive... or to live?" She could no longer silence that question.

The final exam period brought yet another failure. Another "you didn't pass" from a man who saw her as a number, not a person. Dall gathered all the courage she had and went to speak with Professor Naum. She did not go hoping for a miracle, but because she had nothing left to lose. She stood before his desk, notebook in hand, eyes swollen from sleepless nights, and a voice trembling—not from fear, but from a dignity that quietly bleeds.

He lifted his gaze, indifferent, looked at her as if she were just another paper among the hundreds passing through his hands. He said, flatly: "I do not have time to waste. If you have something to discuss, there is a dinner in South Camp—we can meet there, up to you. If not, see you next exam period."

In that moment, something in Dall broke—and at the same time awakened. Something bitter, stripped, yet strong and firm. The breath she drew was no longer a student, but a human being.

"I want to be examined before a commission," she said, clearly and decisively. "I want to see my work. I want to know why I failed."

But no answer came. Only a cold wall. A wall of bureaucracy, vanity, silence, and power in the hands of those who had forgotten that an exam isn't a war, and a student is not an enemy. A wall that let through neither words, nor justice, nor understanding. All she received were closed offices, shrugs, and sentences beginning with: "You know, professorial autonomy..."

That day, Dall understood a hard truth—the system she was in was not interested in knowledge, but in obedience. She realized that she was not the problem. She was not a bad student; she was not stupid or lazy. She was not "not enough." The problem was that she did not fit. That she asked to be seen. That she had the courage to ask questions—and that unsettled them.

Chapter 9

Toward a New Beginning

Donji Vakuf, Bosnia and Herzegovina, 2006. Stormville, NY, US, 2006.

From all of that, the idea of leaving was born. Years of struggle. Quiet, exhausting struggle. As if it were not enough that the world outside was merciless—the inner one was wounded, irreparably. Years of injustice, disappointment, and silent defeats awakened the rebel in Dall.

The very thought that one day her children might walk the same path—her path—tormented her. That they might inherit not a fight for ideals, but a fight for basic dignity. So, she wanted to leave more. To run—not out of weakness, but out of hope. She wanted to find a world where she would not be a stranger.

A place here there were no divisions that tear you apart from the inside—neither by faith nor political belief—but where a person's worth is measured by effort, ability, and what they carry in their heart. She searched for a place to belong. Not a perfect place—just fair enough.

Bitter, hurt, and unwilling to swallow another injustice, to close her eyes for the hundredth time, Dall impulsively rushed into the student services office. She did not think or weigh things. She walked in quickly, spoke briefly, and collected her documents as if by doing so she could erase years of waiting, effort, and hope. When she left the office, for the first time, she did not cry. A kind of peace appeared in her—heavy, slightly bitter, but clean. Because she knew—she owed them nothing more. It was an act of resistance—perhaps even desperation—but in that moment, the only one left to her.

When the dust finally settled, silence remained. And one question. How to tell her mother? How to explain a decision made without agreement, without preparation, without security?

She waged a long, quiet battle within herself. Every sentence she might say sounded insufficient, empty. Panic was breaking her down—but a solution appeared, subtly, almost quietly, like an answer to an unspoken prayer.

An acquaintance from Donji Vakuf had started an au pair agency—a program for girls to go to America to care for children, study, travel, learn the language and culture. The world was there, across the ocean— perhaps not perfect, but different. More open.

Soon after, a school friend studying in Sarajevo contacted her. He offered her the chance to promote the agency in Mostar. It would be an excellent opportunity. A new role. A new beginning. But a question hovered like a shadow over every plan: did she have a backup plan?

Because somewhere deep down, beyond all lists and options, the decision had already ripened within her. She was no longer looking for a way to stay. She was looking to leave—dignified, strong, and, for the first time, in her own name.

After a long inner struggle, countless sleepless nights, and conversations with herself, Dall finally gathered her courage. She packed quietly and calmly and headed home. She did not know how she would tell her mother, had no prepared words or strategy. She only knew that she had to.

While they ate dinner, in the quiet of a daily life she had long felt as a burden, she said it—without preface, without circling around it: "Mom... I want to go to America."

At first, Mira laughed. Briefly, confused as if she'd heard a joke. As if she could not match those words to reality. Then she looked at Dall. And saw that she was serious. She went silent. And she listened.

Dall told her everything—about the feeling of suffocation, the injustice, the exhaustion, about that opportunity that seemed as if it had been created just for her. About the desire to find a world where she would not constantly have to prove her worth. She looked her mother straight in the eyes, her heart pounding as if it would leap out of her chest.

Mira was silent. She did not cry. She did not raise her voice. She did not even want to believe it. Nor to hear it. This was her only child, her everything—how could she let her go across the world?

But if she looked deeper, if only for a moment she quieted her fear, in the very center of her maternal heart, she knew the truth. She knew this might be the best thing Dall could do at that moment. Not because she was running away, but because she was choosing.

Because she dared to ask for more than life had offered her.

And although her heart was quietly breaking, Mira knew—true love does not bind. True love lets go. And prays in silence that everything will be all right.

The rest passed like through a half-dream, half-fog. The days followed one another without clear borders— everything moved quickly, as if someone had pressed fast-forward on a film, and she, in the middle of it all, was only trying to breathe and stay composed.

Preparations began almost immediately. A driver's license—one of the key requirements for leaving. She had never felt the need to drive, but now it seemed like a symbol of freedom, proof that she could steer not just a car, but her own life. She studied with a focus born of deep inner necessity—it was no longer just a test; it was a step toward a new life.

Then—the interview with the family from NY. That video call she would remember forever. Her heart pounded in her throat, her palms were sweaty, and the smile she tried to hold onto was the only shield between her and the strangers on the other side of the ocean. They asked questions, she answered, tried to be honest, warm, capable—because, in essence, that is who she was. In all of it, she felt they were not just asking her to be part of a household, but to step into a world she did not yet know, but that was already opening to her.

And of course—the agency fee. That unavoidable payment that had to be made for everything to officially begin. Behind each figure stood hours of thinking, calculating, quiet help from her mother. Though still uncertain, Mira had already begun to support her, because she knew—when a child wants to fly, you can't hold them on the ground forever.

And so, everything flowed, without a clear sense of time, without enough room for doubt. As if life itself had decided: now or never.

And Dall said— "now."

The original plan was simple, rational—to stay for one year. Long enough to gain experience, learn the language, earn some money, and consider whether to transfer her studies to Sarajevo. Nothing final, nothing definitive. Just a pause. A year to breathe.

Mira, as a mother who—despite her fear—wanted to keep some control over the unknown, gave her one more duty.

"Call your father," she said quietly—almost like an order, but more out of care than strictness.

And Dall obeyed. That conversation would remain etched in her memory forever. It was the first time she had spoken to her father for long, openly, honestly— without pretending, without insecure phrases. As if all the unspoken months and years had condensed into those forty minutes.

He listened carefully, in a silence that was not cold, but full of understanding. Dall spoke quickly, excitedly— about her plans, about the family she would stay with, about the language, the children, about the feeling of finally doing something for herself.

And then, after a long pause, he spoke words that would remain engraved in her memory more than anything else: "You will never come back." She froze. "You will see how people live... what kinds of opportunities they have. Your goals will change," he said softly, then added with a faint smile that concealed sadness: "No matter how much you don't want to hear it, of all my children, you are the most like me."

And although she could not admit it then—not to herself, let alone to him—she knew he might be right.

There was no bitterness in his voice. Only life experience. And the quiet sorrow of a man who knows that some decisions are made once… and leave a mark forever.

Even though they had not been particularly close, having drifted apart years earlier, only much later— when he passed away—did those words remain deeply etched in Dall's memory. But that conversation, that rare moment of honesty, was his gift. Their farewell.

And Dall would never forget it.

Even now her heart tightens and aches every time she remembers her mother's face that morning at the Sarajevo airport. Amid the crowd, the buzz of goodbyes, the embraces, and the silences that speak more than words—Mira stood motionless, as if trying to hold back time.

Her eyes contained everything—sorrow, worry, distrust in a world that was taking her child… but also that deep, unspoken maternal love that does not seek understanding, but only that her child be safe.

Dall remembers that look. It was the look of a woman who had endured much, lost even more, but who stood tall—because she had no choice. Because she must.

In that moment—between clenched fists, unspoken sentences, and eyes that said goodbye without words— Dall felt something she would never forget: the fusion of unbearable pain and immense determination.

Not because she was running. But because she wanted to succeed. At any cost.

Not for herself—but for the children she did not yet have but already carried in her dreams.

Children to whom she would, if she found the strength, give everything she had never been given security, opportunity, choice, peace.

That day at the airport was not an end. It was a quiet vow.

And the beginning of a life that did not come easily— but that was hers.

Everything she had gone through, all the people she had met and who, with their presence, support, and words, strengthened her, had prepared her for this journey—the path of no return, the path that led to her happiness. The path to her choice, her freedom, and her independence. The path to a new, exciting, and brighter life story, filled with hope, possibilities, and faith in a better tomorrow.

Every obstacle, every pain, and every smile were stones paving the road that led her to her true home—the place where she could be herself, where she belonged, and where she could finally breathe with full lungs...

At last, she belonged.

She belonged to him—the one who had been waiting for her all along, somewhere in the silence of distant years yet to come. The one she would truly love with all her being, not with a child's love, but as a mature, capable, and strong woman who always knew what kind of man she wanted by her side—not only as a partner, but as the father of her children, the bearer of security, and of a shared life filled with love and respect.

She had finally found where she belonged—belonging to her children, to the little tender hands that now cling proudly and tightly around their mother's neck, the very ones Grandma Mira so deeply adores. In that embrace, in that quiet safety, she found her home.

A home she built out of dreams, out of tears, out of determination.

A home where she could finally be herself—whole, free, loved.

Amra Mitrovska was born in Bosnia, where she spent her childhood among the valleys of Donji Vakuf and Bugojno—landscapes that shaped her earliest memories and deepest truths. After immigrating to the United States, she settled in the Chicago area, where she continues to build a life rooted in resilience, community, and the quiet strength carried from home.

A lifelong observer of people and emotions, Amra writes stories that bridge her past and present—stories of war, survival, identity, motherhood, and the human spirit that refuses to break.
Her work blends honesty and vulnerability, drawing readers into the intimate spaces where memory and hope meet.

When she is not writing, she is a devoted mother, an advocate for the elderly in her community, and a storyteller at heart—capturing the echoes of where she came from and the path she continues to walk.

www.ingramcontent.com/pod-product-compliance
Lightning Source LLC
Chambersburg PA
CBHW060642130626
46555CB00002B/912